THE BASIC BARNARD: AN INTRODUCTION
TO CHESTER I. BARNARD AND HIS THEORIES
OF ORGANIZATION AND MANAGEMENT

D1067265

This book is dedicated to the growth and development of the Barnard Society, an international organization of students of management who find the works of Chester I. Barnard one of the most useful reference points from which to gain understanding of the development of management thought.

THE BASIC BARNARD:

An Introduction to Chester I. Barnard and His Theories of Organization and Management

by William B. Wolf

ILR PAPERBACK NO. 14

1974

NEW YORK STATE SCHOOL OF INDUSTRIAL AND LABOR RELATIONS, *A Statutory College of the State University,* CORNELL UNIVERSITY

Price: paper $7.50

ORDER FROM

Publications Division
New York State School of Industrial and Labor Relations
Cornell University, Ithaca, New York 14850

Library of Congress Catalog Card Number: 73-620199
ISBN: 0-87546-054-2

SAMPLE CITATION: William B. Wolf, *The Basic Barnard:
An Introduction to Chester I. Barnard and His Theories of
Organization and Management*, ILR Paperback 14
(Ithaca: New York State School of Industrial and Labor Relations,
Cornell University, 1974)

PRINTED IN THE UNITED STATES OF AMERICA
BY
W. F. HUMPHREY PRESS, INC.

Contents

Preface

Chapters

  I. Introduction

 II. A Brief Biography

    The Telephone Company 8
    Public-spirited Activities in New Jersey 14
    The Writing of *The Functions of the Executive* 16
    The United Service Organization 23
    The Rockefeller Foundation 33
    National Science Foundation 34
    Conclusion 37

 III. Barnard's Philosophy and Thought Processes

    Barnard's Humanism 46
    Barnard's Empiricism 49
    Barnard's Speculative Philosophy 54
    Barnard's Framework of Analysis 55
    Conclusion 59

 IV. Concept of Formal Organization

    Barnard's Goals in Writing *The Functions of the Executive* . . . 60
    The Nature of Organization 61
    The Broader Environment of Organization 65
    A Consideration of Individuals in Cooperative Systems 67
        Individuals as Organizational Participants and as
           Whole Persons 67
        Motives 68
        Free Will and Determinism 68
        Efficiency and Effectiveness 69
    Informal Organization 70

  V. Aspects of Formal Organization

    Specialization 73
    Incentives 76
        Method of Incentive 77
        Method of Persuasion 79
    Authority 82
        Authority Defined 82
        The Authoritative Order 83
        The Fiction of Superior Authority 84

Precepts Regarding Authority 85
Insuring the Acceptance of an Order 87
Decisions 90
Logical and Nonlogical Thought Processes 91
The Environment of Decision Making 96
Personal Decisions and Organizational Decisions 97
The Occasions for Decisions in Organizations 98
Evaluation of Executive Decisions 98
The Opportunistic Element in Decision Making 99
Status Systems 101
Functional Status Systems and Scalar Status Systems . . . 102
Devices Used by Organizations to Establish Status 102
The Functions of Status Systems 103
Disruptive Tendencies in Status Systems 104
Organizational Morals 106
Morality Defined 106
Varieties in Business Morality Codes 106
Summary 108

VI. The Functions of the Executive

Providing the Organizational Communication System 111
The Scheme of Organization 112
Executive Personnel 113
The Securing of Essential Services 113
The Formulation of Purposes and Objectives 114
The Executive Process 114
Executive Leadership 115
The Moral Aspect of Leadership 116
Moral Status Compared with Responsibility 117
Conflict of Moral Codes 117
Dealing with Conflicting Moral Codes 118
Responsibility 121
The Sanction of Moral Codes Compared with
Responsibility 122
Organization Personality 122
Barnard's Concept of Responsibility Related to the
Elements of Organization 123

Appendices

Appendix 1: Chronological Listing of Articles, Lectures, and
Manuscripts of Chester I. Barnard 125
Appendix 2: Citation to Accompany the Award of the
Medal for Merit 133

Preface

This book is an introduction to Chester I. Barnard and his concepts of organization and management. It has grown and developed over a period of years. I first perceived the need for this work in 1944 when I read Barnard's classic book, *The Functions of the Executive*. At that time I was a graduate student and shared with my fellow students the difficulty in comprehending what Barnard had written. Over the years I became aware that Barnard's book proved to be obtuse for many professors as well as for their students. Often in informal discussions my colleagues would confess that they found Barnard needlessly abstract, horribly redundant, and extremely hard to follow. I should add that my first reading of Barnard was forced — it was an assignment in a graduate seminar.

The actual writing of this book can be traced to an odd set of circumstances. In 1947 I happened to pick up *The Functions of the Executive* and reread it, guided this time by interest rather than academic assignments. This second reading revealed that Barnard made sense and was eminently profound. *The Functions of the Executive* became my constant companion during the intervening years. In 1961, when I happened to be arranging part of the annual program of the Western Division of the Academy of Management, George Steiner of the University of California at Los Angeles suggested that I invite Barnard to be a guest speaker. Although Barnard was interested in our program he could not participate; he explained that he had "an old man's heart with rusty valves." Because of this I arranged to go to New York and interview him on the story of his thinking.

The interviews were tape recorded and extended over a period of two days. It was in the personal contact provided by these interviews that this book began to take shape. According to Barnard, I was the first to discuss with him his intellectual heritage and his career as well as his more recent thoughts on organization and management. I left the interviews in awe of the man and his accomplishments. I had expected to talk with a businessman-philosopher, but found that he was at the pinnacle of the intellectual world as well as the practical world of management. Most impressive were the man's personal charm, intellectual acumen, curiosity, and humility. He was a humanist who saw in organization the eternal conflict of man in society, but he saw this as providing a contribution to "man" as a whole.

Approximately two months after our interviews Barnard died. During this period I had begun to dig and search for everything he had written. With the help of Peter J. Cabrera, a graduate student at that time, I located a number of Barnard's little-known writings and interviewed several old-timers in the Bell System to learn more about Barnard as a man.

Thus, in 1961, this book was finally conceived. As originally planned, it was to be a simple summary of Barnard's ideas. The research into Barnard's life and works, however, changed my plan, for it revealed richer and richer material. Barnard was not only a philosopher, a practitioner, and scholar; he was also an economist, a statesman, and a person who had significantly influenced American life. He had never sought fame for himself and it was only by reading almost all of his personal papers that much of his life's work could be put together. In fact, a reading of his personal papers revealed that Barnard had written much and thought rigorously about a number of subjects. Thus it became obvious that this book should be an introduction to the man as well as his concepts of organization and management.

It is with humility that I present these materials as an introduction to Barnard's concepts. Although the intention is to summarize, in reality this book is interpretative. Moreover, it should be emphasized that what is presented here is meant to be an appetizer. My goal is to provide background, to distill thought processes, and to present a digest of significant ideas. The basic objective is to interest scholars and practitioners in Barnard's works. Most important, *what appears here is in no way a substitute for reading Barnard in the original.*

In this effort I have been helped by numerous people. First, to Chester I. Barnard I am indebted for personal interviews. Second, I deeply appreciate the help and encouragement given me by Mrs. Chester I. Barnard. In addition, numerous colleagues and graduate students at the University of Southern California have contributed to the evolution of this manuscript. I should also like to express my gratitude to Professors Melville Dalton of UCLA and John Hennessey of the Tuck School at Dartmouth who served as sounding boards for my interviews with Barnard. Professors Russell Taussig of the University of Hawaii, Fred Marrarik of UCLA, and Wilma Stricklin of Northern Arizona State University have helped me clarify my thinking on numerous aspects of Barnard's work. I am particularly in debt to Professor Haruki Iino of Kansai University, Kyoto, Japan, for his shared interest in Barnard's theories and his comments and help with parts of the manuscript. I am also grateful to the Baker Library, Harvard University, for providing me with microfilm copies of their collection of Barnard's personal papers. I wish to thank Mrs. Donald Page, Chester Barnard's niece, for supplying useful information and copies of letters not found in the Baker Library Archives. The quotations from *The Functions of the Executive* and *Organization and Management* are reprinted by permission of Harvard University Press, the President and Fellows of Harvard University.

In writing this book, I owe a significant intellectual debt to Chester I. Barnard. The process of studying and understanding his works has been an invaluable education.

W.B.W.
Ithaca, N.Y.

I.

Introduction

In the various sciences there are key individuals who represent turning points in the search for knowledge. They are symbols of new break-throughs. Their works stand out as significant and guide others in the pursuit of knowledge and understanding. In the field of management and administration one such man is Chester I. Barnard.

In 1938 Barnard published his now classic book, *The Functions of the Executive*.[1] Now, more than thirty-five years later, this book is still one of the outstanding works in its area. It is in its twentieth printing and has been translated into Spanish, Turkish, Arabic, French, Swedish, and Japanese. It is probably one of the most quoted single books in management.

Practically every significant book on management refers to Barnard. Many of the ablest social scientists have publicly acknowledged their intellectual debt to him. His influence can be found in the works of such distinguished men as Lawrence J. Henderson and George Homans of Harvard University, Kenneth Boulding of the University of Colorado, and Herbert Simon of Carnegie Mellon.[2]

Although Barnard is one of the outstanding authorities on organization and management, there is an aura of mystery about him and his work, which stems in part from the scarcity of his publications. He wrote only

---

[1]Chester I. Barnard, *The Functions of the Executive* (Cambridge: Harvard University Press, 1938); hereafter referred to as *The Functions*.

[2]This list is only partial. Barnard's influence is evident in the work of many scholars such as Philip Selznick, Melville Dalton, Robert Tannenbaum, and others. The following acknowledgements suggest the significance of Barnard's impact: Herbert Simon in his book *Administrative Behavior: A Study of Decision-Making Processes in Administrative Organization* (New York: Macmillan, 1958) states that *The Functions* was a major influence on his thinking about administration. In his classic article "The Management Concept: A Rational Synthesis," *Journal of Business* 22 (October 1949): 225, Tannenbaum states that many of his ideas have been influenced by Barnard. There are twenty-three references to Barnard's writings in Dalton's prize-winning book *Men Who Manage* (New York: John Wiley, 1959). In *The Image* (Ann Arbor: University of Michigan Press, 1956) Kenneth Boulding says that one of the books which has most influenced him is the "pioneering work of Chester I. Barnard" (in other words, *The Functions of the Executive*).

one book, *The Functions of the Executive,* and only ten of his articles are readily available.[3] Part of the mystery surrounding Barnard arises from the fact that little is known about the man himself. Few scholars are aware of his total contribution or of the general environment in which he developed his thinking. For many, the major mystery of Barnard involves developing a clear understanding of his ideas.[4] He wrote for the social scientist not for the lay reader. Barnard had an objective which lead him to construct a rigorous, abstract synthesis of the nature of organization and management. *The Functions* is a work which is difficult to read, a work which many students in the field of administration are unprepared to attempt. They have been fed a palatable diet of "readable" text books and against this experience *The Functions* is undigestible. Only those willing to apply themselves and rigorously study *The Functions* are likely to comprehend its significance.

The abstractness of *The Functions* caused many people to urge Barnard to rewrite it in a more readable style. Barnard, however, was uninterested in producing a popular version of his book.[5] He felt that it was folly to attempt to oversimplify subjects which are inherently complex and he held that rigorous study was the answer to comprehending what he had done. His feelings on this matter were expressed in a personal letter written to A. A. Lowman who had urged Barnard to write a more readable version of the book. In replying Barnard wrote:

> . . . Where complex ideas and techniques are involved, as for example in algebra or calculus, it is impossible to get very much from a mere reading of the book. I think it is no less true of a book like mine than it is of mathematics. This means that almost nothing can be gained from a mere cursory reading of it. I would think that, depending upon the man, between five and ten critical readings would be required.[6]

---

[3]Nine of Barnard's articles appear in a volume entitled, *Organization and Management* (Cambridge: Harvard University Press, 1948); hereafter referred to as *Organization and Management.* A tenth article which is relatively easy to obtain is "Elementary Conditions of Business Morals," *California Management Review* 1, No. 1 (Fall 1958): 1–13.

[4]With respect to Barnard's book, Merton J. Mandeville comments that "Barnard's ideas on organization and authority met with considerable disagreement and misunderstanding despite his careful and lengthy explanations. This was to be expected since he was breaking new ground and his concepts were often highly abstract, and at times almost mystical in the true sense of that word." Merton J. Mandeville, "Organizational Authority" in *Current Issues and Emerging Concepts in Management,* Paul M. Dauten, Jr., ed., (New York: Houghton Mifflin, 1962), p. 204.

[5]Although Barnard never attempted such a rewrite, William O. Reeder has. He has written his explanation of *The Functions* and added much illustrative material to make the concepts more concrete. See William O. Reeder, *Variations on a Theme by Barnard* (Syracuse, N.Y.: Privately published by the author, 1959).

[6]Letter of March 23, 1939, to A. A. Lowman, president of Northwestern Bell Telephone Company, Omaha, Nebraska.

INTRODUCTION

Barnard is obviously famous for what he said rather than the style or quantity of his writing. His success is due primarily to his intellectual contribution to the field of organization and management. Before he wrote management theory was dominated by men such as Frederick Winslow Taylor, Harrington Emerson, H. L. Gantt, James Mooney, and Lyndall Urwick. These men were primarily practitioners who were problem oriented in much of their thinking, if not in their writing, and who were introducing scientific method into management. While their contributions were significant in building the field of management, they omitted a broad conceptual framework which allowed for an integration of the field. Moreover, they wrote for the practitioner rather than the social scientist.

Barnard filled this void. He wanted to provide a theoretical framework for the study of management. His approach was philosophic. In a Hegelian manner he began by asking the significant questions and reconstructing the whole before analyzing its elements. In the tradition of William James he emphasized the dynamic nature of organization and management, that is, "the running stream of events."[7] He drew heavily on Vilfredo Pareto to emphasize the differences between what men do and what they say and to conceptualize the organization as a social system. With respect to his organismic or holistic approach to management Barnard was greatly influenced by Kurt Koffka's treatment of gestalt psychology. In short, he developed a conceptual framework in which terms were rigorously defined and concepts were realistically analyzed. In a sense he wrote what might be described as one of the first sociological studies of organization. Most importantly, Barnard was a member of what Karl Mannheim describes as a free-floating intellectual elite. He could objectively observe the society in which he was functioning and he worked at two different levels at the same time. By doing so he could both function as a practitioner and perceive as a social scientist the objective environment in which activities occurred.

It was his focus on social reality which made his book a startling conceptualization. He departed from traditional and historical views and began a new approach. His precise contributions are discussed later in this book; however, the following may be taken as a general list of Barnard's contributions:

1. He was one of the first to emphasize the holistic nature of organization and to relate systems concepts to it.

---

[7]For example, James wrote: "Consciousness, then does not appear to itself chopped up in bits. Such words as 'chain' or 'train' do not describe it fitly . . . it is nothing joined; it flows. A 'river' or 'stream' are the metaphors by which it is most naturally described." In Thorne Shipley, ed., *Classics in Psychology* (New York: Philosophical Library, 1961), p. 168; William James, *Principles of Psychology* (New York: Holt, 1890), vol. 1, chapter 9.

2. He was one of the first to focus attention on the role of the informal aspects of organization.

3. He clearly delineated a general definition of formal organization.

4. He modified traditional belief about the nature of managerial authority.

5. He was one of the first to emphasize decision processes as a significant aspect of organization and management.

6. He drew attention to the nonlogical thought processes in personal decisions.

7. He focused upon the executive organization as a communication system.

This list is cursory. Its details are treated later in this book, but for the present we can recognize why Barnard's work stands out and has had such significant influence. He was the first social philosopher of organization and management and his clear insights dispelled many myths and fictions that were confusing and cluttering conceptualization of management and administration.

II.

A Brief Biography

To understand Chester I. Barnard's concepts of management and organization it helps to study his life. Accordingly, this chapter presents a brief biography to give a feel for the man and the environment in which many of his ideas developed.

Chester I. Barnard was born on November 7, 1886, in Malden, Massachusetts. His parents were frugal and intellectual. The New England attitudes of independence of mind, pragmatism, respect for the rights of the individual, and industriousness were ingrained in him from his early environment.

Barnard's father was a machinist. When Chester was five years old his mother (Mary Putnam Barnard) died leaving him and his older brother, Charles, to be cared for by his father. Fortunately his mother's parents provided a second home for Chester. His maternal grandfather was a blacksmith, and Barnard recalled that he "used to go down and watch his grandfather shoe horses." Grandfather Putnam's home provided a warm environment. There were seven to eight people in it and they "used to argue, endless arguments for hours, on Herbert Spencer and other philosophies" so that at a very early stage Barnard was thrown into the mood of regarding such things as worthwhile, as meaning something, as being lines of thinking that were significant.[1] Thus, the philosophic approach encountered in Barnard's writings can be related to his early childhood. He observed: "that's something you have to get at a very early age or you don't get it. . . ."[2]

Grandfather Putnam's home also provided the environment which encouraged Barnard's interest in music. All of the members of the family sang or played some instrument. Chester studied the piano and became very competent as a pianist.

---

[1] William B. Wolf, *Conversations with Chester I. Barnard*, ILR Paperback no. 12 (Ithaca: New York State School of Industrial and Labor Relations, Cornell University, 1973), p. 8; hereafter referred to as *Conversations*.

[2] *Ibid.*, p. 9.

A significant influence on Barnard's development was his physical inheritance. He was born with poor balance and was very nearsighted. As he recalled:

> One of the things born into me is the lack of proper reflexes for the maintaining of balance. If you're going to throw a baseball, you constantly throw yourself off balance and it has to be automatically corrected. If your reflexes are slow, it doesn't get corrected. The result is, as I dope it out, I was never able to throw a baseball straight and I never was able to hit a golf ball right. There again you're thrown off balance [with] every part of the swing, and that's just something that's innate; but it very much limited my efforts in the field of athletic sports. Plus my eyesight, which is also a limitation. I was pretty nearsighted as a boy and that's a limitation.[3]

These physical handicaps coupled with a remarkable mind and intellectual family environment led Barnard to develop the habit of reading. With respect to this he described himself by saying: "I have always been a voracious reader; not very well organized. I just read an awful lot of books."[4] Not only did he read a variety of books, he also developed the habit of rigorous study. Chester Barnard would read a book four to seven times in order to develop awareness of the author's ideas in all their subtleties. In fact, he maintained the faculty of rigorous abstract study throughout his life. In 1939 he pointed out to a friend that he was studying a book on logic by John Dewey. In his letter Barnard stated:

> Dewey's book is more than five hundred large-size pages. I read that book four times in straight succession, and I shall probably read it several more times in the next three or four years. Despite the fact that I am used to this kind of reading, I do not think I would get much out of it any other way, not because it is badly written — quite the contrary — but because an understanding of it depends upon new points of view and the recognition of subtle distinctions which are of crucial importance.[5]

Barnard's father remarried and there was a child, Chester's half-sister. The family finances remained meager. As soon as Chester finished grammar school he had to go to work. His interest in music led him to a job as a piano tuner and he apprenticed himself to learn this trade. As he recalled: "When I started to learn the trade of piano tuning for three months I got no pay whatever. . . . Then I got $3.00 a week for a while."[6]

---

[3]*Ibid.*, pp. 53–54.
[4]*Ibid.*, p. 3
[5]Letter of March 23, 1939, to A. A. Lowman.
[6]*Conversations,* p. 5.

6

While practicing the trade of piano tuning Chester studied rigorously. Among other things he was preparing himself for prep school. One summer he taught himself Greek and passed the entrance examination of the Mount Hermon School[7] with a 98 score. His entrance to Mount Hermon School was delayed by an illness which was diagnosed as "nervous fever." Barnard described his debility in the following manner:

> I was scheduled to go into the summer semester [at Mount Hermon School]. . . . Well, I had this breakdown [which was called "nervous fever"]. I was then a piano tuner for George Champlin in Boston. I'd been doing a lot of study on my own on the side, rather scattered stuff, law and so forth. And I got sick. I don't know what they'd call it today. I think it's a case where the medical profession when they don't know what anything is give it a name and that fixes it.[8]

Although he could not start with his class, Barnard did get a job working on the school's farm. He was paid $23.00 a month and board. Barnard recalled the situation as follows:

> At that time they had a 1,200 acre farm. I did everything except milk the cows. . . . I did everything else on the farm, and I enjoyed it. I like that sort of thing. I'm naturally a fairly strong person.
>
> * * *
>
> Five o'clock in the morning I was grooming horses. . . . I was pretty sick for two or three weeks. . . . the best thing I could have done was to go to work on the farm, but it was only a very short time before I could pitch a load of hay that was equal to the best of them they had there. Plowing — I loved it. It was a nice team of horses that followed orders.[9]

After attending Mount Hermon School Chester Barnard entered Harvard. He entered in 1906 as a member of the class of 1910. His major was economics and, although he did the work for his degree in three years, he never earned his degree. He explained this:

> Yet I never got a degree because I entered with an entrance condition. I never had any science at prep school so I couldn't take any examinations in physics or chemistry. While I started with a course in chemistry, it was too much. I couldn't carry the load and do all the work I had to do to eat.[10]

Barnard was entirely self-supporting while he studied at Harvard. He earned his living by conducting a dance orchestra and typing theses for other students.

---

[7]Mount Hermon, located in Northfield, Massachusetts, is one of the top-ranking Eastern prep schools.
[8]*Conversations,* pp. 54–55.
[9]*Ibid.*
[10]*Ibid.,* p. 4.

At Harvard Barnard studied languages. He mastered German, French, and Italian. As he recalled in a 1961 interview with the author, "I was interested in language, and the Italian language is beautiful, so I followed it up more than I did German or French. I got so I could speak it pretty freely."

While at Harvard Barnard studied economics under Frank William Taussig and government under A. Lawrence Lowell whom he described as "a fascinating fellow. The greatest anecdotist I've ever seen; he had a story for everything."[11] It was in part due to Lowell that Barnard came to write *The Functions*.

The above is an extremely brief background of Chester I. Barnard's early life. His mother's death, his own physical limitations, and his exceptional intellect tended to set him off and to put him in advance of his years so that he was a loner. He liked to read and study, he loved plowing, a solitary activity, and, as a piano tuner, he worked alone.

It was Chester I. Barnard's isolation from others, his tendency to withdraw into himself and study, that was instrumental in his writing. He was a participant observer; he could participate in an event and at the same time observe it in an impersonal, objective fashion. In his own words

> [being a participant observer is] a very difficult role! It would ruin most men to try to do it. . . . You have to be Dr. Jeckyll and you have to be Mr. Hyde. You have to split your personality, and I acquired a technique for doing it. I never could have written a book if I hadn't done that. No practical manager would write a book like that![12]

The Telephone Company

In 1909 Barnard left Harvard. He had no specific goal in mind other than to get a job and start earning a living. In his effort to find employment he wrote to an uncle who was controller of the Southwestern Bell Telephone System in Dallas, Texas. His uncle suggested that he contact Walter S. Gifford who had been recently appointed chief statistician of the American Telephone and Telegraph Company. Barnard went to see Gifford and was offered a position as a statistician with a starting salary of $50 a month. Thus Barnard began his career with the Bell Telephone System, a career which was to last forty years and to see him rise to the presidency of the New Jersey Bell Telephone Company.

---

[11]Unpublished interview with William B. Wolf, April 5, 1961. Taussig was the author of *Principles of Economics* (New York: Macmillan, 1911), one of the most popular economics books of its era. Lowell, a Boston Brahmin, became a lecturer at Harvard in 1897, a professor in 1900, and president of the University in 1909. He was sole trustee of the Lowell Institute from 1900 to 1943.

[12]*Conversations,* p. 13.

Of critical importance in Barnard's career was his employment by Walter Sherman Gifford. Gifford was a friend of Barnard's, although at the time he hired Barnard their friendship was casual. Mrs. Barnard[13] had known Walter as a boy. In fact, Gifford's father sold lumber and Mrs. Barnard's father bought building supplies from him. Mrs. Barnard recalled that when she was about twelve years old she no longer wanted to take care of her pony so she gave it to Walter. The common interests and background between Barnard and Gifford were the bonds of a long and close friendship. Gifford was born in Salem, Massachusetts, in 1885, one year earlier than Barnard and a scant ten miles from Malden. Gifford entered Harvard one year before Barnard did; both studied economics. Gifford's rise in AT&T was rapid. In 1925 he became president and later was made chairman of the board. Both Gifford and Barnard were active in public affairs and they were members of a number of the same social clubs. Gifford was Ambassador to England from 1950 until 1952. Both he and Barnard were trustees of the Rockefeller Foundation. Like Barnard, Gifford had an academic bent. He read widely and wrote several books.

There is little doubt that Barnard's career at AT&T was favorably influenced by Gifford for Gifford was aware of Barnard's abilities. Moreover, Barnard saw the importance of his relation with Gifford. In *The Functions* he discusses it in general terms under the heading "associational specialization."[14] His point is that knowing the people with whom one works, being used to working with each other, and so forth are most important aspects of a firm's executive organization. In fact, this aspect relates directly to Barnard's discussion of the maintenance of "informal executive organization," Barnard states: "The general method of maintaining an informal organization is so to operate and to select and promote executives that a general condition of compatibility of personnel is maintained."[15]

When Barnard began his job as a statistician at AT&T, the telephone industry was well established. The Bell System had been formed in 1879, and by the time the Statistical Department was set up under Gifford there were approximately one million Bell System subscribers. The service spanned half the nation. The AT&T engaged in a worldwide review of telephone rates and methods. "They kept in touch with what was going on everywhere in the world."[16] Barnard's job was to translate German, French, and Italian and to make studies of foreign rates systems. His training in economics and interest in languages equipped him well for the task. It was a highly technical aspect of the business and was relished

---

[13]Barnard married Grace F. Noera on December 6, 1911.
[14]*The Functions*, p. 131.
[15]*Ibid.*, p. 224.
[16]*Conversations*, p. 5.

by the twenty-two-year-old Barnard. He was soon recognized as an expert on telephone commercial practices and the economics of telephone rates. His expertise in this area lead to his being appointed during World War I to be a technical adviser on rates to the state commission and operating board of the United States Telephone Administration. Within AT&T Barnard was promoted to the position of commercial engineer in 1915.

Barnard graduated from the study of foreign telephone systems to become an expert on rate systems in this country. He spent much of his time giving seminars to executives in the Bell System companies. In this capacity he was a central headquarters staff man. One of the advantages of the job was that he was brought into contact with the entire Bell System. He was able to see the company as a whole and his specialty involved concern for the whole organization.

One event which helps to understand Barnard as a person occurred during this time. As Barnard recalled it,

> [A]lthough I was just a young cub[,] I reported to Vice-President [H. B.] Thayer, who became president of the AT&T and who was at the time president of the Western Electric Company also. A very able, very fair, and broadminded fellow. The question was what to do about a new rate system for the city of Detroit. A man named [B. E.] Sunny was president of the company which gave service in Michigan. . . . He had no use for this young whippersnapper highbrow; he didn't accept any recommendation that I made. He had ideas of his own, and the top management of AT&T thought they had to go along. . . . Mr. Thayer said to me, "Can't you modify your report in certain directions to harmonize with Mr. Sunny's view?" And I said, "Look, Mr. Thayer, you men at the top managing this thing can and must take into account many considerations that a staff man working on one section of a problem can't deal with. They are beyond my ken. Of course you can do what you want to, but what you are asking me to do is alter my statement of what my beliefs are. The minute you do that, if I accede, you destroy my usefulness. You just make me a yes man. I think you ought to go ahead and agree with Mr. Sunny if that's what you think is the wise thing, but I don't think you ought to involve me in doing that. I've made my report and I stand by it." And [Mr. Thayer] said, "My boy, you're right!" But he might have said, "You're an SOB and the hell with you." There's no way of avoiding that kind of risk. The people who haven't got guts enough to face it, just finally don't have guts enough to do anything.[17]

Thus, early in his career Barnard took risks involved with decision making and had the courage to stand by his conclusions. He was no yes man.

---

[17]*Conversations,* pp. 42–43.

For slightly more than his first ten years with the Bell System, Barnard was in a staff (rather than line) position. It was this experience which helped him formulate his position on the relation of line to staff personnel.

In 1922 he moved to Pennsylvania to become assistant vice president and general manager of the Bell Telephone Company of Pennsylvania. At this time Barnard made one of his earliest contributions to the Bell System's literature on organization, a short article focusing on the improvement of the functional organization.[18] (The term "functionalized" was used as a synonym of "specialized.") He argued that improvement must proceed along three lines. First, a cooperative attitude between functional units must be maintained; second, adequate interdepartmental instruction must be established; and, third, the cross training of personnel should be promoted to ensure an adequate supply of executives. Each of these ideas can be related to portions of Barnard's theory of organization discussed in chapters IV and V of this book.[19]

The style of this early paper is much looser than later Barnardian writing. Yet one central point, which Barnard developed often in later works, is that the executive should be exposed to a wide range of activities so he can see the company as a whole. At the time the Bell System had a special program called JET (an acronym for Junior Executive Trainees). It was a well-developed training-rotation program for men of promise.

In 1925 Barnard gave his second paper on management topics. This paper was delivered at (Dean Sackett's) Industrial Conference at Pennsylvania State College and the topic was the "Development of Executive Ability." This paper is the precursor of many things Barnard wrote later; moreover, it is the earliest paper to show the later Barnardian style. The writing is tight; terms are carefully defined; and, by synthesis, Barnard establishes the executive task, arrives at the essential qualifications of executives, and suggests what can be done to develop executives. Of interest are the six universal qualifications for executives which Barnard lists. They are the ability to determine the desirable results to be accomplished in any business or activity; ability to organize; ability to state intelligibly the things required of the organization; ability to secure enthusiastic cooperative action; balance; and flexibility. Parts of the general theses found in this paper were to be developed in *The Functions* and in his 1945 talk to faculty members of the School of Business and the Division of Social Sciences of the University of Chicago.[20]

---

[18]"Business Principles in Organization Practice," *Bell Telephone Quarterly* 1 (July 1922).

[19]See pages 60–110.

[20]This talk was published as "Education for Executives," *Journal of Business* 18 (October 1945): 175–182; it is represented in *Organization and Management*, pp. 194–206.

Barnard believed that the first three qualifications could be developed by general and special educational methods. He pointed out that, while general intellectual capacity is not, in itself, sufficient to produce executive ability, education tends to develop the faculty of intelligent discrimination. Barnard, however, believed that the qualifications of leadership, balance, and flexibility were least susceptible to development by formal training. He saw these "as perhaps natural aptitudes strengthened and greatly matured by experience, and especially by opportunity to exercise them in executive positions."[21]

As to fundamental training for developing executives, Barnard said, " . . . other things being equal — I should be much inclined to favor engineering training over training of other types for two reasons: First, this type of training calls at an early stage for precision in mental processes; and second, because it involves quantitative methods and statistical processes. *Quantitative measurements and statistical analysis are becoming more and more important as parts of the management machinery.*"[22]

Barnard saw four basic methods for the formal training of executives in industry, which were closely akin to the ones advocated in his 1922 paper on principles of organization: training by conferences where management problems are discussed; the use of staff positions for the study of special aspects of management problems and their application to particular conditions; rotating of men of management ability from one type of work to another; and special intensive instruction.

Barnard's rise in AT&T was rapid. In 1922 he became assistant vice-president and general manager of the Bell Telephone Company of Pennsylvania. He became vice-president of that company in 1926. At forty-one he was made president of the New Jersey Bell Telephone Company. Regarding his job at the Pennsylvania company Barnard recalled:

> . . . the constitution of the state of Pennsylvania had prohibited a consolidation of telegraph companies, and telephone was classified legally as a telegraph. One of the little independent companies up in the western part of the state broke that by judicial decision. It was determined that if any company gave up its telegraphic rights, per se, it could consolidate with any other company provided this was done before the district court, and so forth. That release had just been made. At that time the state was ridden with duplicate telephone systems, most of which were in very bad shape. It became my job to buy and sell proper-

---

[21]Chester I. Barnard, "The Development of Executive Ability," manuscript, 1925, p. 2.

[22]*Ibid.*, p. 4. Emphasis added. It should be pointed out that in his 1945 talk Barnard changed his emphasis for training executives. He no longer leaned toward engineering, but instead emphasized training in the humanities and science so that executives could understand what goes on in the world and human relations.

12

ties to effect consolidations and to create monopolistic service in each of these communities, very much to the public's relief. It's just a false idea to have competition in a thing like telephone. So I was very much engaged with that sort of thing, also in building and rearranging and readapting the organization, which is an endless job — you never get away from it. Conditions change and they change rapidly; if you are properly alert you begin to mold the organization to fit the conditions.[23]

At New Jersey Bell Telephone Barnard was also concerned with building the company. In describing his work he stated:

That was a job of amalgamating two entirely different organizations. The southern part of the state, by which I mean Princeton and South Tom's River and south, was owned by a company known as the Delaware and Atlantic Telegraph and Telephone Company. It was a part of the Pennsylvania organization; I was the operator of it. Then we set up the new company. That involved taking, or using, the old as the vehicle for effecting the consolidation, which involved the purchase of all of the property in the northern part of the state from the New York Telephone Company, which at that time operated in New Jersey and New York. My job was to amalgamate the two organizations which had, you know, different backgrounds. . . .

[It was a] very fascinating kind of thing to do because you're dealing not only with differences in tradition, you're dealing with differences of personality and differences in training and outlook. The New York Telephone Company was dominated by the ideas that are essential to the operation of a complete big city. The other company was operating in a large number of small places. The New York Company has small places, too, but the dominant thing necessarily was the big city with all its complications and techniques. That's the kind of problem that you have with amalgamation.[24]

In response to a question about the operational procedures used in merging these two companies, Barnard replied:

Well, of course, one way is appointments as the opportunity for them comes up. You transfer people from one section to the other and, after awhile, that dominance of a particular tradition or a particular background of personalities begins to disappear. The second thing is that you're constantly preaching to the organization. An executive is a teacher; most people don't think of him that way, but that's what he is. He can't do very much unless he can teach people. He does not do it by any formally organized classes or seminars, but that's what he has all the time. He has conferences that are seminars in which either he or

---

[23]*Conversations*, p. 6.
[24]*Ibid.*, pp. 6–7.

other people who are involved do the instruction and teach themselves. That's absolutely essential. You can't just pick out people and stick them in a job and say go ahead and do it. You've got to give them a philosophy to work against, you've got to state the goals, you've got to indicate the limitations and the methods.[25]

Public-spirited Activities in New Jersey

It was Barnard's position in the telephone company that helped put him into prominence in New Jersey public affairs. He recalled:

... I had to do a lot of public talking as a representative of the telephone company, and I had to keep off practical issues that were controversial. That forced me into dealing with abstract subjects and trying to make them interesting to the audience. I got away with it. Most speakers at rotary clubs and chamber of commerce meetings and things of that sort really haven't got a damn thing to say and they don't say it; they spend a lot of words on it. Whereas many of the public are easier to get through a philosophic approach to the problems they are concerned with, and they will listen.[26]

Barnard had a deep interest in youth. This was reflected in his being a member of the board of managers of the New Jersey Reformatory for Boys as well as his being a member of the "Committee of One Hundred" sponsoring the National Boys Club movement. In addition, he was a national sponsor of Air Youth of America and a member of a special committee appointed by the Secretary of Labor to study the problems of children.

A measure of the scope and variety of Barnard's public service activities can be gotten from a 1936 biographical sketch:

One of the major telephone undertakings of recent years, that of creating a telephone system of wide range and flexibility to meet the peculiar and difficult service problems in the Northern New Jersey metropolitan area, was launched under his direction. His interest in the orderly development of this area led to active participation in various important activities outside the telephone business. Among these are the Regional Plan Association, Inc., of which he was a director and member of the executive committee (1931–1935); the New Jersey State Regional Planning Commission (1931–   ), and the Committee on Population Redistribution of the Social Science Research Council (1934–   ). His recognition of the importance of human relations in social welfare, as well as in industrial management, has led to his giving unstintingly of his energies and ability in many directions. At the request of Gover-

---

[25]*Ibid.*, pp. 7–8.
[26]*Ibid.*, pp. 45–46.

nor Morgan F. Larson, he organized New Jersey's Emergency Relief Administration in October 1931 and directed this work for eighteen months before turning it over to other hands. When a reorganization was sought in April 1935, the New Jersey Relief Council was formed and he was recalled by Governor Harold G. Hoffman to serve as its chairman, and also as relief director until the reorganization was effected. He withdrew from these activities in November 1935. In the organization of the New Jersey Relief Administration, Mr. Barnard established methods and practices which have since been incorporated in the relief administration of a number of other states. His knowledge and experience gained in relief work led to his appointment to the Committee on Relief Expenditures and Activities of the United States Chamber of Commerce (1934), and to the Social Science Research Council Committee on Social Security (1935–   ).

As examples of Mr. Barnard's active interest in the problems of human relations may be cited his services as Vice-President and Member of the Board of Managers of the New Jersey Reformatory (1929–1935) and as a director and member of the Executive Committee of the National Probation Association (1934–1935).

The responsibility of the citizen, and particularly the business executive, to aid the community and nation with counsel and leadership as opportunities present themselves has often been accepted by Mr. Barnard. For four years (1930–1934) he represented the district comprising New Jersey, New York, Pennsylvania, and Delaware as director of the United States Chamber of Commerce. When Newark's municipal finances caused concern, he served on the Citizens' Advisory Finance Committee (1932–1935) to help restore them to a sound basis. He gives his energy and support to worthy charitable organizations, and serves regularly as a leader in the yearly Community Chest campaigns in Newark. He was a member in 1934 and 1935 of the directorates of the Hospital Council of Essex County, and the Homeopathic Hospital, East Orange (1933–1935). Mr. Barnard represents New Jersey in the National Economic League, is a director and member of the executive committee of the new Newark University, and is in charge this year [1936] in New Jersey of Harvard's campaign to raise funds for the endowment of professorships. A musician of ability and student of music, he is president of the Bach Society of New Jersey and is on the advisory board of the New Jersey Musical Foundation.

Mr. Barnard is a director of his own company, of two large insurance concerns, and of two of New Jersey's largest banking and mercantile establishments.

A significant recognition of the man in the telephone industry is his selection (1935) by telephone veterans throughout the country to serve as president of their organization, The Telephone Pioneers of America.

Mr. Barnard's election to the Newcomen Society of England is another indication of his great interest in affairs outside his own industry.[27]

In his later years Barnard turned down honorary degrees from a number of the nation's outstanding universities, including the University of Chicago and the University of California. He felt the honor was empty because "the academic community has no use for honorary degrees."[28]

The Writing of The Functions of the Executive

As with so many things in life, the writing of *The Functions of the Executive* developed from a complicated and unpredictable set of circumstances. Barnard had no intention of writing such a book.

Barnard's activity in public affairs led him into academic circles. He was active as a guest speaker at conferences at the Wharton School of Finance and Commerce of the University of Pennsylvania and he served on a number of visiting committees at Harvard. While Barnard was at Harvard, Dean Wallace Brett Donham, dean of the Harvard Graduate School of Business at that time, introduced him to Lawrence J. Henderson of the Harvard faculty. It was through his friendship with Henderson that Barnard was encouraged to assemble his ideas about organization and management. Henderson held the Lowell Professorship of Chemistry at Harvard; he was also chairman of the Society of Fellows and foreign secretary of the National Academy of Science. Barnard described him as follows:

> . . . he was a Brahmin. He was intellectually quite arrogant. . . . He didn't suffer fools gladly, but he was highly respected by scientists. He was the foreign corresponding secretary with the National Academy of Sciences and really had a first-class mind. He was not an experimentalist, always claimed he was too lazy; but he was responsible for the creation of two or three laboratories. At the time I knew him, although he had no official position on the faculty, he had an office over in the Business School; and he was working around there on seminars and several other efforts.[29]

The bond of interest between Barnard and Henderson centered on the work of Vilfredo Pareto. Barnard had read the French edition of Pareto's

---

[27]C. I. Barnard, *Mind in Everyday Affairs: An Examination into Logical and Non-Logical Thought Processes* (Princeton, N. J.: Princeton University Press, 1936). The biographical sketch appears in the introductory material to this address which was delivered at Princeton University on March 10, 1936.

[28]Unpublished interview with William B. Wolf, April 5, 1961.

[29]*Conversations,* p. 2.

sociology, *Traité de sociologie générale*.[30] With his characteristic rigor Barnard had read this several times and had a thorough grasp of what Pareto had said. Henderson had come upon Pareto quite late in life. Barnard described Henderson's interest in Pareto:

> Nobody that I know of at Harvard ever fell for Pareto as hard as Henderson did. He got way out of balance on that. Pareto was very stimulating and worthwhile and had things to say, but he was nowhere near the fellow Henderson thought he was. That's an interesting psychological history. . . .

> Henderson was utterly convinced that there was no possibility of any science, strictly, in social relations. He held to that view until 1925, along in there, when he wrote a book on the physical characteristics of blood.

> In writing that book he had to deal with certain characteristics of blood, of properties of blood, under conditions of renal disease and kidney troubles of various kinds. In order to get anything he wanted, he had to work with the staff of the Massachusetts General Hospital. As a result of this contact with those men he became convinced for the first time, I think in his life, that men with clinical experience acquired an intuitive knowledge that was not available in any other way and that while it might not be called science it couldn't be called nonscience either. These fellows were able to predict what was going to happen under various conditions; and they couldn't explain how they could predict it, but it was based on what he called intuitive familiarity with the subject. That opened his mind quite a bit.

> There was an entomologist at Harvard whose name I cannot at the moment recall, . . . who Henderson thought was the best-read man he ever knew. He was not a scientist, but was really a very learned and a very capable fellow in the fields of zoology and so forth. He said to Henderson one day, "You ought to read this book by Pareto!" Henderson said, "I'm not interested in reading what Pareto or anybody else has to say about the social system." Now I should preface that remark by saying that Henderson was one of the best-read men in literature, German and French literature particularly, that I've ever known. It was not because of lack of interest in the humanist side of things, but he just separated the two spheres completely and absolutely. This man said, "But Pareto's different. I think you will find that it is very much worth your while to read Pareto's Sociology." Henderson did, and became captivated right away because Pareto's got a lot of physics and mechanics and chemistry and that kind of approach. . . . That's what got Henderson excited about it. Then he got into some disputes with other people about it, especially with a cousin of his who was a profes-

---

[30]Vilfredo Pareto, *Traité de sociologie générale* (Paris: Payot, 1917–19).

17

sor at Yale, Yandell Henderson. He got himself into a polemic position where he was fighting everybody all of the time on behalf of Pareto.[31]

Barnard became a close friend of Henderson. He worked with him in the development of a special course at the Harvard Business School, Sociology 23. In a letter to Dr. Harold W. Dodds, president of Princeton University, Barnard explained his relation with Henderson:

> I have collaborated with Dr. Henderson quite extensively in development of his lectures, and the problem which he deals with is one on which we have both done considerable work together. That problem is to present a reconciliation between the strictly intellectualist's view of what ought to be human behavior and the practical and realistic view, namely that human behavior is chiefly governed by sentiments accompanied by profuse rationalizations which, as any administrator learns, are usually necessary, and often useful, accompaniments of social action.[32]

Barnard's friendship with Henderson led to his writing *The Functions*. He recalled how this came about:

> Lawrence Henderson was a very close friend of A. Lawrence Lowell. Lowell was president of Harvard. He and Henderson used to walk back from Boston to Cambridge from the medical school and the college. They talked about many things, and they were very close friends. Well, Lawrence Lowell was the sole trustee of the Lowell Foundation, and [he] had to arrange for this lecture series. . . . Of course, Lowell was always looking for suggestions as to who they could get, and Henderson suggested that he get me. He gave me complete freedom as to what I should talk about and whether I should take six lectures or eight.
>
> When I was a boy in Boston I used to go to Lowell Institute lectures. They were open to the public, and they were very popular then. By the time I gave my lectures they were not popular at all. Nobody ever attended Lowell lectures. I don't believe there were more than fifty people ever in my audience and half of them were my friends and relatives.
>
> So I agreed to do it; I picked out the functions of the executive and took eight lectures to do it. I had to travel back and forth every week from New York to Boston.

---

[31]*Conversations*, pp. 16–17. Yandell Henderson was professor of applied physiology at Yale from 1921 to 1932. The entomologist was William Morton Wheeler (1865-1937), the author of several classics in social behavior among insects, including *Ants: Their Structure, Development and Behavior* (1910), *Social Life Among the Insects* (1923), and *Demons of the Dust: A Study of Insect Behavior* (1930).
[32]Letter to Harold W. Dodds, May 2, 1941.

18

[Dumas] Malone, historian of Columbia, was the head of the Harvard Press. He knew nothing about the lectures, but he thought maybe the Press ought to be doing something with Lowell Institute lectures. He asked Arthur Page, who was then a vice-president of AT&T and a friend of mine and was on what they called the Syndic of the Harvard Press, a board of directors, if he would introduce me — which he did. Malone convinced me to convert these lectures into a book.[33]

Thus it was that Barnard came to give the Lowell lectures and these were published in book form. [See Henderson's letter to Lowell and Lowell's invitation to Barnard on pages 19–21.] In reflecting upon the sequence of events Barnard wrote a friend:

> . . . like so many other things we do in life, this is one which I never should have undertaken had I known in advance what I was getting into. I was, of course, most pleased to be invited by Ex-President Lowell of Harvard to give the Lowell Institute lectures, particularly because he was an old professor of mine and one of the most practical-minded men I have known of. As my invitation was months in advance of the lectures I had ample time to do a serious subject. Then I was requested by the Harvard University Press to work the material up into book form just as I was giving the first or second lecture and was red hot, so I agreed to do it, thinking it much easier to do than it proved to be. All in all this manuscript was written completely, I think, sixteen times and there is scarcely a word in it that has not been thoroughly weighed. Even so, but for the assistance of a professional critic in the Harvard Press — a lady who knew nothing whatever of the subject — it would not have been so presentable as it is.[34]

January 23, 1937

Dear Lowell:

Mr. Chester I. Barnard is president of the New Jersey Bell Telephone Company. I first heard of him a year ago when somebody showed me a lecture that he had given at Princeton on "Mind and Everyday Affairs". Since then I have seen two or three other things that he has written, and yesterday I had two long talks with him.

Barnard has been thinking clearly and effectively about the larger aspects of his experience and seems to me to have reached a stage where he

---

[33]*Conversations*, pp. 14–15. Arthur W. Page was an author in his own right. He wrote a short history of AT&T called *The Bell Telephone System* (New York: Harper and Brace, 1941). Dumas Malone, the biographer of Thomas Jefferson, was director of the Harvard University Press from 1936 to 1943. In 1945 he was appointed professor of history at Columbia University.

[34]Letter to A. A. Lowman, president of Northwestern Bell Telephone, March 23, 1939.

has not only said important things but where he has a great deal more of even more general character to say. In fact, he has now in mind a large book that is to discuss in the most general manner and from a scientific point of view what is loosely called nowadays in the business world organization.

It is my impression from what he has written and from yesterday's conversation that he stands almost alone among men of affairs as a greatly respected executive and a clear thinker about abstract problems. To be sure, he is occasionally awkward in expression (I don't mean rhetorically) and he hasn't the facility and virtuosity in managing his thinking about abstract questions that he would have achieved if that had been his principal business in life. But, unless I am mistaken, he is a first-rate all round human being and a man of remarkable intellectual power.

These remarks are here set down on paper because it occurred to me that you might think him well qualified to give Lowell lectures and that in spite of the obvious difficulty for him of arranging to do so, he might be willing and able, if you wished it.

Yours very sincerely,
(L. J. Henderson)

A. Lawrence Lowell, Esq.
171 Marlborough Street
Boston, Massachusetts

March 10, 1937
Dear Mr. Barnard:

I have read with great interest both your "Mind in Everyday Affairs" and "Methods and Limitations in Foresight in Modern Affairs", by both of which I am much impressed; and in accordance with the suggestion of Professor Henderson I am writing to ask if you can give, during the season of 1937–1938, a course of six or eight lectures at the Lowell Institute. I thought this might be a chance to put into more systematic form the philosophy, so to speak, of these two addresses.

Of course these addresses are particularly interesting to me because I have thought along somewhat similar lines; and if I were not eighty years old I should want to extend my "Conflicts of Principle" by some suggestions and illustrations about administration, whereof I have had experience in a somewhat peculiar but illuminating field; to wit, that of attempting to change the atmosphere of a university.

I ought to add that the lectures at the Lowell Institute come at the rate of two a week (Monday and Thursday, or Tuesday and Friday) during the period of the course, the first course beginning early in October and the last ending in March. I ought also to add that the honorarium is one hundred dollars a lecture.

Yours very sincerely,
A. Lawrence Lowell

Chester I. Barnard Esq.
540 Broad Street
Newark, N.J.

Barnard delivered his Lowell Lectures extemporaneously. His ideas on the subject, however, had been gestating for a number of years. For example, in an unpublished rough draft of the preface to *The Functions*, Barnard wrote:

> In June 1936 I delivered a commencement address entitled "Some Persistent Dilemmas of Social Progress." An extended manuscript used as a basis for this address had the sub-title "An Approach to the Social Sciences from the Viewpoint of the Arts of Organization." Friends urged me to publish the manuscript, but as it was not in [a] form satisfactory to me I began a rewriting of it. It then seemed to me that the word "organization" which recurred throughout might mean less or something different to those who had little experience in the management and development of organization than to me. Upon further reflection I was not sure I knew what I meant myself, and I was certain that the reduction of my conception to intelligible language was a matter of no small difficulty. I thereupon abandoned the revision pending an effort, which has proved a long one, to describe what I mean by "organization". This book is the final outcome of it.[35]

The Functions was immediately recognized as a significant contribution to the literature on organization and management. Much of its early popularity was with friends from Harvard University. Harvard professors such as Henderson, George C. Homans, Elton Mayo and Philip Cabot were impressed by this philosopher-practitioner, and Barnard was invited to discuss *The Functions of the Executive* at a Conference of the Committee on Work in Industry of the National Research Council. Barnard met with this group on February 28, 1939. A thorough abstract of the book was published in proceedings of the conference.[36]

---

[35]Unpublished personal notes of Barnard.

[36]Henderson was chairman of the committee. The secretary was George C. Homans and Elton Mayo was also a member. The proceedings of the conference were published as Committee on Work in Industry of the National Research Council, *Fatigue of Workers: Its Relation to Industrial Production* (New York: Reinhold, 1941), pp. 137–160.

An interesting critique of *The Functions* was written by Melvin Copeland of the Harvard Graduate School of Business Administration. Copeland challenged Barnard's conceptual scheme and his general theoretical treatment of the subject. Barnard immediately wrote a rejoinder to Copeland which stimulated a great deal of interest in his book.[37]

Barnard did not expect *The Functions of the Executive* to do well. Its sales started slowly, but gradually built up and as of 1961 the book was doing better than it had ever done. Regarding its success, Barnard observed:

> Well you get very strange results. There's a man named John B. Clark, who is the head of what was originally the Clark Thread Company, textile operators. I know him because we were both directors of a fire insurance company. He is a hard-boiled, tough guy, the last man I would suppose would be interested in anything I would write. On account of World War I he never went to college. He went into the Army and when he got through he didn't want to go back. He bought a dozen copies of my book to distribute to his friends. The lawyer, I can't thing of his name now, who was chairman of the board of directors of Chrysler Corporation, also bought several copies to distribute to his friends. Now these are matters of surprise to me.[38]

In attempting to evaluate the impact of *The Functions*, Barnard observed: "It apparently is used as required reading, I wouldn't say as a textbook, all over the country and a good deal in Europe. . . . Something that is quoted all the time, especially after it's survived twenty-odd years, is having some influence, but you can't put your finger on it."[39] Despite its wide use Barnard stated in 1961 that "There's been no follow-up as far as I'm concerned. I haven't pursued the thing."[40]

A review of Barnard's writings after publication of *The Functions* shows that he did refine and enlarge upon some of his concepts. The three areas he developed were the nature of leadership, the role of status systems in operating organizations, and the nature of business morals.[41]

It should be pointed out that Barnard wrote only one book and miscel-

---

[37]M. A. Copeland, "The Job of the Executive," *Harvard Business Review* 18 (Winter 1939): 148–160; Chester I. Barnard, "Comments on the Job of the Executive," *Harvard Business Review* 18 (Spring 1940): 295–308.

[38]*Conversations*, p. 46.

[39]*Ibid.*

[40]*Ibid.*, p. 47.

[41]See the Stafford Little Lecture given at Princeton University on April 25, 1939, and reprinted under the title "Dilemmas of Leadership in Democratic Process," in *Organization and Management*, pp. 24–50; and "The Nature of Leadership" written in 1940 and based upon lectures given to the Chemical Reserve Officers of the Second Corps Area, United States Army, January 24, 1940, and to the Week End Conference of Business Executives at the Harvard Graduate School of Business Administration, March 9, 1940. This essay has been reprinted in three sources: Schuyler D. Hoslett, ed., *Human Factors*

laneous articles. From 1938 until the time of his death he gave many talks but only published thirty-seven papers which received varying degrees of circulation. In addition to leadership, status systems, and business morals he turned his attentions to "Observations and Reflections on a Brief Call at Leningrad and Moscow,"[42] planning for world government, general economics, and the control of atomic energy.[43]

Probably one of the reasons for Barnard's limited number of publications was that in 1945 he began the monumental intellectual task of editing the papers of his friend L. J. Henderson. Barnard wrote several drafts of an introduction to the Henderson materials. Although he believed that he had completed the job, he never submitted the manuscript for publication. In reply to the question of why he had not released these materials Barnard stated that there were "various reasons." One upon which he enlarged was that (Henderson) got himself into a polemic position where he was fighting everybody all of the time on behalf of Pareto. . . . in his ardor of behavior regarding Pareto, he was off balance considerably. . . ."[44]

The United Service Organization

Until shortly before his death, Barnard had only slightly changed his concepts as they were developed in *The Functions*. He pointed out that

In Management (N. P.: Park College Press, 1946); *Organization and Management*, pp. 80–110; and William B. Wolf, *Management: Readings Toward a General Theory* (Belmont, California.: Wadsworth, 1964), pp. 82–100. "Education for Executives," *Journal of Business* 18 (October 1945): 175–182, has also been reprinted in *Organization and Management*, pp. 194–206. "Functions and Pathology of Status Systems in Formal Organization," a lecture given at the University of Chicago, Human Relations in Industry Seminar on August 15, 1945, has been reprinted as Chapter Four in William F. Whyte, ed., *Industry and Society* (New York: McGraw-Hill, 1946), and pp. 207–244 in *Organization and Management*. "Ethics and Modern Organization" was an address given at Bloomfield College and Seminary Convocation Dinner in East Orange, New Jersey on November 8, 1945. See also "The Elementary Conditions of Business Morals," *California Management Review* 1 (Fall 1958): 1–13. For a chronological listing of Barnard's speeches, lectures, manuscripts, and published materials see Appendix 1.

[42]Published privately in South Orange, N. J., September 11, 1939, by Barnard.

[43]*Concerning the Theory of Modern Price Systems and Related Matters*, a letter to Barnard's daughter, Frances, was written March 10, 1941, and privately published by Barnard in South Orange, N. J., in 1941. "On Planning for World Government" is in *Approaches to World Peace*, Lyman Bryson, Louis Finkelstein, and Robert M. MacIver, eds. (New York: Conference on Science, Philosophy and Religion in their Relation to the Democratic Way of Life, 1944); and in *Organization and Management*, pp. 134–175. Barnard's review of Barbara Wooton's book *Freedom Under Planning* appeared originally in *Southern Economic Journal* 12 (November 3, 1946): 290–300, and was reprinted in *Organization and Management*, pp. 176–193. "International Control of Atomic Energy" was an address delivered to the Controllers Institute of America on September 12, 1946, and reprinted for the Great Island Conference, New York, January 1947; a talk to the Great Issues course at Dartmouth College, "Atomic Energy Control," is available in the *Dartmouth Alumni Magazine*, February 1948.

[44]*Conversations*, p. 17.

until 1946 he had not adequately treated the nature of status systems. "I had left out of my book if not Hamlet, perhaps Ophelia, and did not discover it for seven years — and no one reported the omission to me!"[45] Significantly, he changed his emphasis. He felt that *The Functions* put too much emphasis upon "authority." "In my opinion, the greatest weakness of my book is that it doesn't deal adequately with the question of responsibility and its delegation. The emphasis is too much on authority, which is the subordinate subject."[46] The development of this point of view can be traced to Barnard's experience during World War II. Barnard was president of the United Service Organization during the period of its greatest development, 1942–45. Regarding this experience Barnard observed:

> The presidency of the USO was one of the toughest jobs I have had, and one from which I learned a great deal, especially with respect to responsibility without authority. . . . It was a *very* difficult job and I was at it for three years. It turned out very successfully, though after I'd been in for a few months I thought it was going to be a *complete* failure.
>
> * * * * *
>
> It was very much needed. The aspect of it the public never will get is that it maintained cohesion in communities. It gave them an outlet, something to do. There were thousands of women who passed out coffee and did every kind of thing, including a lot of menial labor, who had sons in the Army and Air Force and Navy. The USO was a safety valve for that, plus the fact that it gave a means for coordination and cooperation in the community where otherwise there would have been a dozen different efforts which would mostly become futile because they would be so small or so uncoordinated.[47]

Barnard described his central problems at the USO as follows:

> . . . there were six agencies involved in this general operation, and five of them had religious backgrounds or overtones. The sixth, the Travelers Aid Society, had no religious connotations. If you let them talk about *why* we would do something, you split into a thousand splinters. The Catholic idea of why you do anything is completely different from that of the others and so on. But if you could focus attention on the utility of the specific thing, they could all agree. Now, it was an organization that has used through the years a million or two volunteers. The paid organization was really very small, but it had 600,000 volunteers at the peak. The handling of volunteers is a quite different thing from the handling of a paid organization; and in many respects volunteer

---

[45]*Organization and Management*, p. xi.
[46]*Conversations*, p. 15.
[47]*Ibid.*, pp. 33, 37.

service, while it's indispensible for a good many things, is the most expensive way to do anything. The volunteer creates a kind of an obligation in the minds of a lot of people, and you can't fire an incompetent volunteer without repercussions. Whereas in the case of a paid employee, you frequently can get repercussions. You have to take account of it, but it isn't the determining factor. But here's John Jones, or Mrs. John Jones, which is better, who's devoted night after night, or day after day, to running a snack bar or that sort of thing, and she isn't competent. She doesn't do the right job. But if you pull her off —.

* * * * *

On the other side, I was in constant difficulty with the military authorities who really controlled. We couldn't do anything that was not acceptable. If we sent people out of the country, as we did in the USO camp shows — we gave shows all over the world — they had to be cleared by the military. Every individual had to be cleared by the military. Usually that involved another clearance by naval intelligence, and it usually involved clearance by the state department. It got to be a damned complicated business, but I still had to carry on. In the second place there was a lot of information that we needed to manage the thing that we couldn't get, due to the secrecy requirements. And that which we could get was so delayed that our decisions at any particular moment — well, that element is involved in all operations. But of course it's much stronger in the religious organizations or a thing like USO or particularly a military organization or in a tightly knit organization with a whole body of dogma, and so forth, such as the Communists have and such as the Catholic Church has than it is in a business organization.[48]

In dealing with these problems Barnard recalled:

The only thing you could do if you had a difficulty was to persuade the military authority that this was something that should be done from the standpoint of military efficiency. You didn't get very far with most military officers in talking about community aspects. The top echelons would be aware of that, but in a most general way, and wouldn't really know how to apply it. The military authorities are really dependent on the civilians for doing this kind of job, but they never appreciate it. They did give a good deal of recognition to it, but after it had struggled through. Initially, when I first went into it, . . . they thought it was just another damnfool organization of do-gooders. You had to fight that kind of thing.[49]

---

[48]*Ibid.*, pp. 33–34 and 36–67.
[49]*Ibid.*, p. 37.

His USO expérience had a significant effect on his concepts. In fact it caused Barnard to change his emphasis in discussing authority and responsibility:

> . . . my experience at USO *really* developed my present concepts! It's a case where the full organization really operated on a moral basis. There was no economic accomplishment involved at all. The only attention that you had to pay to economic factors was raising the money, and the money never was very great and finally it reached 60 million dollars a year. Considering the scope (we operated over 3,000 clubs at one time), it was really little, but it was feasible only on the moral basis of acceptance [of responsibility].[50]

Barnard's effectiveness as president of the USO has been recognized by many. When he was elected president, the USO had 692 units and was established as a vital force in the war effort. As Barnard took over, a campaign to raise $32 million was launched and was oversubscribed. In 1943 USO ceased its own money raising and became a part of the National War Fund which united the fund raising of many war-related philanthropies into one annual nationwide campaign. Barnard acted as director of the National War Fund from 1943 until 1946. Under Barnard's leadership, the USO developed a network of approximately 3,000 units serving the armed forces within this country and in fourteen overseas areas with entertainment and recreational services. One estimate held that 30 million servicemen were served each month by the USO.[51]

Barnard believed that one of the most difficult undertakings of the USO was related to integration of minority groups, especially Negroes. At one time he stated: "We [the U.S.O.] have demonstrated that it is possible for us to perform a united service without relinquishing our special philosophy and points of view to make a total America. In the long run this accomplishment may be more important than anything we have done, for unity amid diversity is a fundamental problem of world peace."[52]

Barnard's USO experience brought him into contact with numerous illustrious Americans. One of these was John D. Rockefeller, Jr. In fact Rockefeller had been one of those urging Barnard to accept the USO presidency. The following letters describe the growing admiration which Rockefeller had for Barnard. On April 9, 1942, he wrote to urge Barnard to accept the presidency:

---

[50]*Ibid.*, pp. 34–35.
[51]*Current Biography 1945*, p. 36.
[52]*Ibid.*, p. 37.

April 9, 1942

Dear Mr. Barnard:

I am sending this note to be given to you after your talk with the USO representatives.

I want you to know how earnestly I hope you will accept the presidency of the organization in spite of whatever sacrifices it may involve. When the greatest military hero of the day, General MacArthur, says, regarding the men who fought so bravely at Bataan: "To the weeping mothers of its dead I can only say that the sacrifice and halo of Jesus of Nazareth has descended on their sons and God will take them unto Himself", can there be any question but that spiritual force alone will win this war if it is to be won?

There is no organization in the field equipped to do this task, other than the USO, that approaches morale building from the spiritual point of view. This does not mean prayer meetings or church services necessarily. It means the kind of life on the part of the workers — professional and lay — who have contact with the soldiers, that springs only from a spiritual background and belief.

If I had the youth, the strength and the ability which you have, I would count it as the highest privilege of my life to head this organization and make it the effective force for winning the war which it is capable of being made but of which it will fall short without such leadership as you can give it. Very earnestly I plead for your acceptance of this invitation.

Most sincerely,
John D. Rockefeller, Jr.

Mr. Chester I. Barnard
Kindness of Mr. Robertson

Rockefeller's growing respect for Barnard is captured in an interchange of letters between Raymond B. Fosdick and Rockefeller.[53]

---

[53]John D. Rockefeller, Jr. (1874–1960) was on the executive committee of the USO and in this capacity was involved in finding a new president for the organization. He was a trustee of the Rockefeller Foundation from 1913 to 1940 and chairman of the board from 1917 to 1940. Raymond Blaine Fosdick, a New York lawyer, was a trustee of the Rockefeller Foundation and General Education Board from 1938 to 1948.

May 5, 1943

Dear Mr. Rockefeller:

We had a meeting of the Joint Army and Navy Committee in Washington yesterday, and Chester Barnard made a report on the U.S.O. that was, to my way of thinking, a model of what such a report ought to be. He was as detached and objective as if he were completely outside the U.S.O. He told us its strong points and its weak points and where they were located. The Committee was deeply impressed and I believe he made more friends for the organization than we have had in our group before. He certainly established himself in the respect and the confidence of the crowd down there. They have always liked him but they had never really seen him in action before.

I am passing this along because I am sure you will be interested to know the impression he made.

Sincerely yours,
(sgd) Raymond B. Fosdick

Mr. John D. Rockefeller, Jr.
30 Rockefeller Plaza
New York City

May 14, 1943

Dear Mr. Fosdick:

Your letter of May 5th regarding Mr. Barnard's report at the meeting of the Joint Army and Navy Committee is most gratifying. I am glad that you are beginning to see, as I have during this past year, what ability and what a fine character Mr. Barnard has, how wholly detached he is in his analysis of problems, how quick he is to see and criticize the faults in his own organization and how generous in his appraisal of other groups.

Because I knew it would be greatly appreciated by Mr. Barnard, I have taken the liberty of sending him a copy of your letter.

Very sincerely,
John D. Rockefeller, Jr.

Mr. Raymond B. Fosdick, President
The Rockefeller Foundation
49 West 49th Street, New York City

Rockefeller's respect for and admiration of Barnard is further reflected in his letter of February 6, 1945.

February 6, 1945

Dear Mr. Barnard:

I thought your speech at the USO luncheon yesterday a masterpiece of its kind. It was brief; you spoke of many subjects; the subjects were selected with great wisdom and discretion. The singling out for honorable mention of two of the paid executives was wise and just. Your expressions of appreciation to the Army, to the Navy, to the officers and board, to the workers and to the givers were well deserved and the language in which your remarks were presented was beautifully chosen.

I would be proud were I able to conceive and write anything approaching as fine an address of its kind, but you made the address extemporaneously. I take my hat off to you.

How profoundly the service you have rendered the USO these past years has been appreciated by those who know what that service has meant to the organization and the cause, and who also know what it has cost you, you will never begin to know.

Please do not think of acknowledging this note, which I am sure you know comes from my heart.

Very sincerely,
John D. Rockefeller, Jr.

Mr. Chester I. Barnard, President
The USO
350 Fifth Avenue, New York City 1

January 28, 1948

Dear Dr. Barnard:

Dr. Kimball recently sent me the final printed report of the USO. Since in my acknowledgment of it and in the expressions of appreciation for the service which it reported, I was really addressing both you and Dr. Kimball, will you permit me to repeat in this letter what I said to the Doctor.

"What an extraordinary report it is both in the service rendered and in the cleverness of its presentation! I can well imagine what an immense amount of time must have been required on the part of a number of people to prepare a report so extensive, so attractive and so easy to read. It is a model of its kind and I congratulate you and your staff on it.

But in referring so fully to the form of the report, please do not think I am overlooking the character and volume of the service rendered. You and Mr. Barnard are entitled to the everlasting gratitude of the six constituent organizations and their associates in the work for an able, devoted, tireless, and unselfish leadership that in both instances has been unique.

As I looked at the curve in the chart which showed the rise of the activities of the organization and then the much more rapid fall, I found it difficult to say whether the task of building, baffling as it was, or the task of liquidating, with all its perplexing problems, was the more taxing. But without trying to decide that question, one can say without qualification that both tasks were performed with consummate and outstanding skill.

How grateful I as a former member of the Executive Committee am personally to both of you gentlemen for the service you have rendered in this war enterprise, I cannot adequately express in words. Not hundreds but literally thousands of intricate, complex, trying problems you have, both of you, yourselves worked out, bringing to the Executive Committee invariably, with the problem, the solution which practically without exception was approved and adopted by it. But in what you have done you have, both of you, been serving your country and the men and women in the armed forces. Your reward has been the knowledge of what the service has meant to millions of men, than which there could be no better reward."

Although I have on various occasions undertaken to tell you of my gratitude for your service to the USO, that gratitude is frequently in my mind nor can the repetition of its expression ever adequately indicate the depth of my feeling or do justice to my deep sense of obligation for what you have done for the USO.

> *Ever gratefully,*
> *Your friend,*
> *John D. Rockefeller, Jr.*

Mr. Chester I. Barnard, President
New Jersey Bell Telephone Company
540 Broad Street
Newark 1, New Jersey

For his USO service Barnard was awarded the Presidential Medal of Merit. He also received numerous letters of commendation, among them letters from General George Marshall, chief of staff of the War Department; James Forrestal, secretary of the Navy; Henry L. Stimson, secretary of the War Department; T. J. Watson, president of International Business Machines; Fleet Admiral E. J. King of the United States Navy; the executive board of the Young Men's Christian Association; and others. The general tone of these commendations is summarized by the memorial resolution passed by the board of governors of the USO in 1961 at the time of Barnard's death:

> Mr. Barnard came to the USO at a time when its need for basic organizational planning coincided with the crowded military events which followed Pearl Harbor. His talent for organization was reflected in the expanded service to the nation's armed personnel beginning with less than seven hundred USO facilities and rising to some two thousand seven hundred facilities throughout the various war areas, where USO met the welfare and morale needs of some fourteen million men and women called into the service of our country. . . . His service to the nation in support of the armed forces won Mr. Barnard the Presidential Medal of Merit. His contributions to the foundation and development of the USO are well-nigh immeasurable.[54]

It should be mentioned that in 1943, while serving as president of the USO, Barnard was the civilian member of the Naval Manpower Survey Committee in the Third Naval District. For this service he was awarded the Navy's Meritorious Civilian Service Award in August 1944.

Barnard's contact with Washington was frequent and longstanding. In 1937 Secretary of Labor Frances Perkins appointed Barnard to a committee to study the problems of the older worker in industry. (Older was defined as over forty years of age.) In 1941, before World War II, Barnard served as Assistant to Secretary of the Treasury, Henry Morgenthau, Jr. In 1948 Barnard served on the Committee on the National Security Organization established by the Hoover Commission. (This was part of former President Herbert Hoover's study of the reorganization of the executive branch of the federal government.) In 1955 Barnard served on another "Hoover Commission," then as a member of the Task Force on Personnel and Civil Service.

No sooner did Barnard give up the presidency of the USO (he stayed on as a director and member of the executive committee) than he accepted a three-month appointment as consultant to the director of the federal Office of Scientific Research and Development. In this capacity Barnard served on the Committee on Atomic Energy chaired by David E. Lilienthal. The committee's report on the international control of atomic energy was judged the best publication of the year in the field of International Relations by the Committee on Awards of the American Political Science

[54]Letter from A. Lincoln Lavine, general counsel for the USO, to Peter J. Cabrera, November 22, 1961.

Association.[55] While serving on this committee Barnard came to know and respect both Lilienthal and Robert Oppenheimer.[56] The report of the Lilienthal Committee became the basis of United States policy. Secretary of State James F. Byrnes commented on it in the following letter to Barnard:

March 23, 1946

My dear Mr. Barnard:

The Under Secretary of State as Chairman of the Committee on Atomic Energy which I set up on January 7, 1946 transmitted to me on March 17, with its unanimous endorsement and comments, the final report of your Board dated March 16. I am greatly impressed with this document. I share the view of my Committee that it is the most constructive analysis of the question of international control that has appeared and that it provides a definitely hopeful approach to the solution of the entire problem.

I have sent the document to the President, to Mr. Baruch, to the Secretary of War and to the Secretary of the Navy and I have also transmitted it to the members of the Senate Special Committee on Atomic Energy. In doing this, I have expressed my strong view that the intensive character of the work which this document reflects and the high qualifications of the men who were concerned with it, make it a paper of unusual importance. I have urged that it be given the most serious study and consideration by the Government of the United States and I hope that it will shortly be possible to make the document public for I believe that it provides the most suitable basis for the informed public discussion which is one of the essential factors in the development of sound policy.

I want you to know of the appreciation of the Department of State and of my personal gratitude for the devotion and the disinterestedness which has characterized the unique public service which your Board has performed. As occasion arises, I hope that we may call upon you for further assistance. But, I am mindful of the sacrifice that you have had to make in order to serve on the Board, not only in personal effort but in laying aside the heavy responsibilities which each of you has in your regular work

---

[55]Chester I. Barnard, J. R. Oppenheimer, Charles A. Thomas, Harry A. Winne, and David E. Lilienthal, *A Report on the International Control of Atomic Energy* (Washington, D. C.: GPO, 1946).

[56]Both men were to come under political attack. Barnard publically supported Lilienthal who was being considered to head the Atomic Energy Commission in February of 1947.

and you may be assured that we shall not call upon you unless it is essential in the public interest.

I am enclosing for your information a copy of the letter which I have sent to Mr. Walter S. Gifford expressing my appreciation to the American Bell Telephone and Telegraph Company for relieving you of your regular responsibilities sufficiently to make it possible for you to engage in this public work.

Sincerely yours,
James F. Byrnes

Mr. Chester I. Bernard,
   President, New Jersey
     Bell Telephone Company,
      540 Broad Street,
       Newark, New Jersey.

Enclosure:
  Letter to Mr. Gifford.

After the report of the Lilienthal Committee, Barnard became active in public discussions of atomic energy and was appointed consultant to the American representative on the United Nations Atomic Energy Commission.

The Rockefeller Foundation

In 1948, after nearly forty years with the telephone company and more than twenty years as chief executive of New Jersey Bell Telephone, Barnard became president of the Rockefeller Foundation. He had been a member of the board of trustees and of the executive committee of the foundation since 1940. He succeeded Raymond B. Fosdick who was retiring. Undoubtedly Barnard's USO experience, especially his friendship with John D. Rockefeller, Jr., influenced his decision to move to the foundation. On March 3, 1948, Barnard resigned his presidency of New Jersey Bell, but was promoted to chairman of the board of the company. He served as chairman until June 30 when he assumed his duties at the Rockefeller Foundation; Barnard had been on the executive committee of the foundation since 1940.

In reflecting upon the work of the Rockefeller Foundation Mr. Barnard observed:

> The aim of the Foundation as expressed by the founder, or in the charter, was to do anything for the welfare of mankind. I never could get a

definition of what that phrase meant from anybody. It's again another thing like the USO: if you're dealing in abstractions you can get no agreement. But you had no trouble in getting an agreement among the people concerned at the top (the trouble was with the public) in the desirability of eliminating hookworm, which is the first thing they tackled (before the foundation was established it was attempted by another organization) or malaria or any of the contagious diseases, yellow fever, typhus, typhoid, and all the rest of them. The concrete results of that effort makes an appeal to almost everybody, except for a few who think it's an outrageous interference with nature and that people ought to be allowed to die easily or painfully, whichever way it may be. But you can't get most people to play it that way. On the other hand you have great difficulty getting the public to go along with essential methods if they cost very much. Fortunately, malaria, which is not very widely controlled, is completely controlled in this country and in Western Europe. It can be handled without great expense; even in India it should be handled without great expense.

* * * * *

The Rockefeller Foundation didn't do any work itself if it could avoid it. The support of most scientific research in medicine and physics was farmed out, so to speak. We supported others, and others were really the final judges of accomplishment and competence. When it came to some of the diseases like yellow fever, the universities were not equipped, were not willing, or were not able to conduct the required research. You can't get research done by just saying you want it done and here's a hundred million dollars to do it. You've got to find the guy that's really interested in doing it and competent to carry it on. Most of its effort is in supporting things and supporting people who are deemed promising. That's the only word you can use is promising, because you have to support research. There's always a gamble.[57]

National Science Foundation

Barnard reached the mandatory retirement age of sixty-five and was succeeded in the foundation presidency by Dean Rusk, but he was soon appointed chairman of the National Science Board of the National Science Foundation. The National Science Foundation had been established by the Congress in May 1950 to cultivate and appraise scientific research efforts and to advise the executive and legislative branches of government on the allocation of federal funds for research. Barnard's role in this endeavor was summarized by President Dwight Eisenhower in his response to Barnard's letter of resignation.

---

[57]*Conversations*, pp. 38–39.

January 27, 1956

Dear Dr. Barnard:

In view of the compelling personal reasons you stated in your recent letter, I must regretfully accede to your request to resign from the Board of the National Science Foundation. I understand that the Director of the Foundation has discussed with you the importance of certain problems to be considered by the Foundation in the next few months and that you are willing to postpone to March 1, 1956, the effective date of your resignation. I am thankful for your readiness to do so.

As a charter member of the National Science Board and as its Chairman for the past four years, you have played a leading part in the development of a closer relationship between the Federal Government and scientific activities. The importance of the role of science in the future of our country and, indeed, of mankind, is ever more apparent. I am deeply grateful that the Foundation could draw upon your experience and wise counsel during these critical years.

With best wishes for your happiness and well-being in the years ahead,

Sincerely,
Dwight D. Eisenhower

The Honorable Chester I. Barnard
52 Gramercy Park North
New York 10
New York

Probably one of the most significant occurrences during Barnard's term as chairman was in connection with the International Geophysical Year. Barnard's comments are reflected in his exchange of letters with President Eisenhower.

June 22, 1954

The President
The White House
Washington, D.C.

My dear Mr. President:

I wish to convey to you the sincere appreciation of the National Science Board for your wholehearted support of this country's program for the

International Geophysical Year as presented in the budget request which you have sent to the Congress.

As you know, there are pressing problems of interest to agencies of the Government and to the nation, as well as to the scientists in the field of geophysics, whose solution primarily depends upon simultaneous observations throughout the world. It is heartening that in times like these so many nations have agreed to cooperate in a worldwide program on scientific matters of interest and concern to all. It is eminently fitting and indeed important that the United States join the other nations in this effort, and that the Federal Government accept responsibility for our participation.

With grateful acknowledgment of your support in this important undertaking, I am

> *Faithfully yours,*
> *Chester I. Barnard*
> *Chairman*
> *National Science Board*

bc: Director, Bureau of Budget
Dr. Hauge, The White House

June 24, 1954

Dear Dr. Barnard:

I appreciate your letter with respect to the United States program for participation in the International Geophysical Year.

I am glad to support this undertaking. It is a striking example of the opportunities which exist for cooperative action among the peoples of the world. As I understand it, some thirty nations will unite their scientific resources for a simultaneous effort, extending over two years, to penetrate the basic geophysical forces which govern the natural environment in which we live. Under especially favorable conditions, scientists of many nations will work together in extending man's knowledge of the universe. The findings of this research will be widely disseminated throughout the world, aiding in the further development of telecommunications, aviation, navigation, and weather forecasting. It is doubtful whether any single nation could undertake such a program. Acting in concert, each participating nation, contributing within its means, secures the benefits of the program.

The United States has become strong through its diligence in expanding the frontiers of scientific knowledge. Our technology is built upon a solid foundation of basic scientific inquiry, which must be continuously enriched if we are to make further progress. The International Geophysical Year is a unique opportunity to advance science, while at the same time it holds the promise of greater technological gains both for ourselves and for other nations. I am sure that our participation in this far-reaching effort will very materially strengthen our bonds with the many cooperating nations and make a constructive contribution toward the solution of mutual problems.

Sincerely,
Dwight D. Eisenhower

Dr. Chester I. Barnard
Chairman
National Science Board
National Science Foundation
Washington 25, D.C.

Conclusion

The above is a brief, and incomplete, summary of much of the life and work of Chester I. Barnard. It fails to portray fully the dynamics of Barnard's personality. He was a scholar, a philosopher, an executive, and more. He was a man vitally involved with the affairs of the world in which he lived.

Barnard's reputation as a clear analytical thinker led John Foster Dulles to encourage him to attend the Commission on Durable Peace sponsored by the National Council of Churches. Barnard had an influence on the National Council of Churches. Through a peculiar combination of circumstances he was instrumental in the council's effort to increase Americans' self-awareness of how our society functions.[58] In recalling how his influence on the council came about Barnard commented:

> This thing originated in the fact that the people of the council wanted to make some kind of studies. I had, on two or three occasions, pointed out that the attitude of the theological people was unrealistic. They didn't know what they were talking about when they were talking about the economic system or the business system or the social system — which is a much better word, economic is too narrow and too limited. They talked with Paul Hoffman, former president of Studebaker.

---

[58]Several books, which were all published in New York City by Harpers, came out of this effort. They included *Goals of Economic Life* (1953) edited by Alfred Dudley Ward; *The Organization Revolution* (1953) by Kenneth E. Boulding; *Social Responsibilities of the Business Man* (1953) by Howard Bowen; *American Income and Its Uses* (1954) by Elizabeth E. Hoyt *et al.*; *Christian Values and Economic Life* (1954) by John C. Bennett *et al.*; *The American Economy, Attitudes, and Opinions* (1955) by Alfred Dudley Ward; *Social Responsibilities and Farm Leadership* (1956) by Walter Wilcox; *Social Responsibilities of Organized Labor* (1953) by Neil W. Chamberlain.

He said he would undertake to raise some money for the purpose if I'd help. I came over to New York here and met him and we talked about it. My advice to the council was, at this stage at least, to get all the money you can from foundations which are the most neutral source that you can find. They went to work on that basis. Quite unexpectedly, it was one of those things that you never can count on, I became president of the Rockefeller Foundation. The application for funds for this thing came in shortly after I was elected. So with hope for my own proposition, so to speak, I put it through, and we made two large appropriations. It was quite effective in its influence on a limited number of theological people, including John Bennett and Reinhold Niebuhr, because they gathered, in the course of this, a lot of very competent academic people. Not very much from the world of affairs. This examination of the social system partly grew out of John Foster Dulles' request that I help keep their feet on the ground at the meeting of what was then called the Commission on Durable Peace at Cleveland, and I suppose the participants were about half clergymen and half civilians. I said to an Episcopalian Bishop, "I listened to this discussion, and you're talking about a world I don't know anything about. I live in this world that you are talking about, but it isn't at all like what you say it is."[59]

Bernard's interest in public affairs is evident. The following memo, from his personal files, indicates that he was concerned and involved with trying to improve this country's relations with the Soviet Union. The memo was written in 1950 and the parties to whom it was distributed are not listed.

STRICTLY CONFIDENTIAL

Memorandum

Several weeks ago Dr. Willits said that Mr. Clarence Pickett, who has been connected with the American Friends Service Committee, was trying to set up an occasion on which Mr. Malik of the Soviet Delegation of the United Nations could meet two or three leading businessmen. Willits asked if I would be willing to consider the matter and I said I would. Accordingly, somewhat later Mr. Pickett came in to talk with me about it. I told him that I would be willing to join the group provided I would be assured that the proposed meeting was at least not unfavorably regarded by the State Department and that the appropriate officials of that Department should be reminded that I had been a member of the State

---

[59]*Conversations*, p. 40. Paul Gray Hoffman was president of Studebaker Corporation from 1935 to 1948 and became chairman of the board in 1953. Well known for his public service, he was a member of the United States delegation to the United Nations from 1951 to 1953 and was a trustee and chairman of the Committee on Economic Development.

BIOGRAPHY

Department panel concerned with the problem of the International control of atomic energy. The subject has evidently been discussed with and through Dean Rusk, Assistant Secretary of State, and I was assured by Mr. Pickett that though the undertaking was in no sense an official one, it was agreeably regarded as a possible means of the development of a reconciliation of the conflicting interests of the two countries, also that there was no exception to my being a member of the group.

Some weeks passed before arrangements could be made agreeable to all concerned and finally I was advised that the meeting would take place at luncheon on Sunday, November 19, at the residence of Mr. Lancaster. I had met Mr. Lancaster several months ago at a very small conference of Quakers led by Mr. Pickett to discuss the Soviet-U.S. relations in general. Lancaster is head of the legal firm which serves as the counsel for the National City Bank. He has an exceptional acquaintance with Soviet officials and a great deal of knowledge of Russian affairs. He is now seventy-six years old, but looks and acts not over sixty-five.

The party to be assembled was to consist of Frank Abrams, Chairman of the Board, Standard Oil Company of New Jersey; Charles E. Wilson, President of the General Electric Company; Henry Ford, II, President of the Ford Motor Company; Mr. Pickett; and myself. It was uncertain whether Mr. Malik would bring anyone with him. Mr. Pickett, Mr. Abrams, and myself were picked up by Mr. Ford's limousine at the Pierre Hotel at eleven o'clock. Mr. Wilson was flying down from Syracuse or Schenectady to be met at the airport by Mr. Ford, who was driving his own car, and we met at some road junction not far from Manhasset where the Lancasters' residence is.

We arrived at the Lancasters' shortly after twelve o'clock and Mr. Malik turned up in a Cadillac limousine about one o'clock. He was accompanied by a young man whose name I could not note and have forgotten. He was the son of a former Soviet diplomat located in Washington and had attended the Quaker school there. His English was excellent. Although Mr. Malik speaks English fairly well, apparently for the purpose of this meeting the young man was to serve as a translator. He took shorthand notes during most of the meeting, apparently to aid in translating Mr. Malik's statements which were frequently so long without interruption for translation as to make such notes really necessary for that purpose. But I was of the opinion that another purpose was to make a record on the spot.

Mrs. Lancaster had prepared a semi-buffet luncheon of hot turkey and vegetables followed by a salad and a light desert. Because of the character of the meeting, no servants were present at any time, and Mrs. Lancaster served the meal and removed the dishes, etc. We sat about with little tables on which our plates could be rested.

Mr. Wilson was used to start the discussion by our asking him to repeat the proposal which he had previously made publicly at the Riverside Church in New York. This was that some twenty-five or more Russians of different statuses and callings should be placed in the United States on farms, in factories, etc., for periods of three, six, or more months and that a corresponding number of Americans of different statuses and callings should simultaneously be similarly placed in Russia. (This is somewhat similar to the scheme of John H. Finley, Spencer

Miller, et al., in the late 20's and early 30's under which German students were brought here for a year to be located in the factories and on the farms of the United States. I did not mention this because a check-up after the war had shown that only one of the students brought over under this plan had turned Nazi and he under duress, i.e., I did not wish to give the suggestion that this plan would have an ideological slant.) Mr. Wilson's thought was that in this way both people could learn better what was the real state of affairs and thinking and points of view in the two countries. Obviously this is a rather fanciful idea in the sense that the limited numbers involved could hardly affect opinion and understandings in either country in any short period. It served, however, as a basis for discussion.

One of the interests involved was the Russian assumption, or at least statement, that American industrialists were war mongers and that they were the scions of an aristocratic class perpetuating a class condition for their own advantage. It was emphasized by all that American business is almost unanimously opposed to war as destructive of its own interests and that leaders of American industry for the most part had risen from the bottom. This applied to Messrs. Pickett, Abrams, Wilson, and myself, the only exception being Mr. Ford.

Mr. Malik set forth the reasons for Soviet hostility as arising from the creation of military bases by the United States in Europe and elsewhere, the proposals to drop bombs and start war made in some of the wild statements, presumably referring to Secretary Matthew's speech, General Orville Anderson's famous talk, etc., and specifically referring to the most recent belligerent positions of secretary Acheson. On the other side Malik recounted some of the history of Russia which he said through the centuries had been invariably attacked by others, whereas Russia never had gone to war except in self-defense. Finland was not mentioned. He said that Stalin had several times expressed the belief that the two systems could live in the same world, that Russia did not want war, and that it had no desire to disrupt the governments of other countries. The reference was to interviews with Stassen, Johnson, and others. All of this material evidently is very thoroughly organized in the mind of Malik, and he is able to call chapter and verse very readily. The tendency of the discussion was to spin off into generalities of the kind that go on in United Nations debates, and it was useful from time to time to pull it back to the concrete suggestion of Mr. Wilson.

We offered the opinion that the conviction of the American people would from now on depend upon deeds rather than words, and I offered the belief that it was obviously necessary that if any such plan was adopted it should not be a one-way plan, i.e., delegations from both countries should be exchanged. I also offered the thought that the psychological effect of admitting a group of Americans for this purpose as indicating a raising of the Iron Curtain would, if it could be accomplished, have a very powerful effect on opinion in this country. At one point Mr. Malik suggested that the paucity of comfortable facilities, etc., would involve for Americans a degree of what they might call hardship and perhaps would not be acceptable for this reason. He was assured that this would not be a factor in the possibility of the plan.

He put the shot at one time rather adroitly in saying that he knew that 90%

of the people of this country owned property, that the standard of living for practically all classes was higher than anywhere else, that he therefore wondered why we seemed to fear Communism so much under the circumstances. He also said everything that happens in this country that we regard as adverse or that happens in other countries, e.g., Latin America, was attributed to the Soviets or to Communists. Thus, if we have serious labor trouble it was assumed to be stirred up by the Communists, whereas the fact is that before there was any Russian Revolution we had had similar trouble on a large scale more than once. No doubt he had in mind the I.W.W., the Knights of Labor, the great Pullman strike, etc. He could have said that revolutions had been chronic in Latin America, also, before there was any Soviet regime. There was no specific discussion of the Comintern and the Cominform though this would have been relevant to any statement that the Soviets were not concerned with disrupting the systems in other countries.

Mr. Lancaster — who said little — very wisely, I thought, at the proper stage had suggested that preliminary to the attempt to put into effect Mr. Wilson's plan, a visit of some twenty-five leading industrialists, small businessmen, labor leaders, etc., would be an excellent way to begin.

At about four o'clock, that is after about three hours of discussion, Mr. Malik gave the signal to depart by saying that he regretted that the need for translation had prolonged the conference perhaps unduly, that he regarded the matter as worth considering and that of course it would have to be considered by higher authority.

Malik is the son of a Ukrainian peasant, somewhere around forty-plus years of age, looking very much like a prosperous middle class business executive in the United States. He was Soviet Ambassador to Japan during the war and was there, of course, when the atomic bombs dropped. I believe he was subsequently counsel at the Soviet Embassy in Washington. He is evidently very clear headed, was entirely agreeable and not belligerent, and has a sense of humor. There were a half a dozen good laughs during the conference. He was well aware of my background, and on my being introduced to him, he referred to the fact that I had been on the atomic energy panel.

This kind of thing is, of course, a shot in the dark, but as I told Mr. Pickett, any other specific proposal would have the same quality. No panacea makes any sense as a starting point in this sort of undertaking. Only some concrete proposal which, if adopted, might serve merely as a starting point for understanding and reconciliation means anything. This meeting was in effect sought by Mr. Malik to secure a contact with leading industrialists. My impression is that probably the Soviet authorities are aware that what they get from Communist intelligence reports and from reading the statements of and about businessmen in this country are not adequate means of acquiring full information. He asked at one point to what extent such men as we were could be regarded as in a position to express the attitude of American businessmen generally. I offered at this juncture the opinion that so far as the desire to establish amicable relations with the Soviets and to avoid war was concerned, I was certain that this group represented the predominent opinion of the business community, but that in the present state of exacerbation of international relations probably a great many American business-men would be today exceedingly skeptical of the sincerity of the Soviet repre-sentatives in stating that the Soviets did not wish war and were not undertaking to disrupt the governments and societies of other countries.

To meet what were thought might be the exigencies of the situation, the Lan-casters served cocktails and sherry though they never before served cocktails in this residence which has been theirs for thirty years. I was told that Mr. Malik declined a cocktail, drinking orange juice, attributing his declination to the fact that he had heart trouble, and Mr. Pickett assured me that this was not an excuse but that he did in fact have such trouble.

Shortly after Mr. Malik and his associate had departed the rest of us also de-parted, Mr. Ford, who was staying on Long Island, driving off in his own car, his chauffeur-driven car taking to New York Mr. Pickett, Mr. Abrams, Mr. Wilson, and myself. We disbursed from Grand Central Station at about 5:20.

While it seemed to me, and I think to all of us, that the probabilities of any specific developments coming from this meeting were pretty low, it nevertheless seemed not to be a useless meeting. I have the distinct feeling that at the present time the Soviets would like to be conciliatory and at least to mark time for the time being. I have no doubt that there is a certain degree of possible misjudg-ment due to the exaggeration of columnists, politicians, etc. There is also no doubt that a number of the things that we do inadvertently make the sincerity of our protestations questionable in the minds of the hardboiled Soviet officials, but for anything like a wise appraisal of the essential situation one would need to have highly confidential information in the possession of the FBI and the general and military intelligence organizations. I suppose that no American present had such resources available to him.

Chester I. Barnard

November 20, 1950

The fact that Barnard inspired faith and loyalty is evidenced by many of the tributes paid to him. When he resigned from New Jersey Bell Tele-phone the directors of the company wrote the following letter to Walter S. Gifford, then president of AT&T.

August 7th, 1945

Mr. Walter S. Gifford, President,
American Telephone and Telegraph Company,
195 Broadway,
New York, N.Y.

Dear Mr. Gifford:

The Directors of the New Jersey Bell are desirous of honoring our Presi-dent, Mr. Chester I. Barnard, by procuring at Company cost a portrait of himself, to be executed by a competent artist. It is needless to say that the suggestion does not proceed from him and is not unusual in character, but he is mindful that the New Jersey Bell Company is a unit in a wide-flung national system. He tells us that he knows of no precedent in the system for the expenditure of money for such a purpose, and feels that you should be consulted as to the propriety of our Company's approval. I am deputed by my associates to bring the matter to your attention.

In New Jersey Mr. Barnard is not merely the President of the New Jersey Bell Telephone Company. He has been the executive head of this public service organization from its beginning and during his tenure has directed its affairs with dignity, ability and general approval. He came to us a stranger, but, during the now more than twenty years of residence among us, has built for himself, quite outside of his business relationship, a position of importance in the City and State and in the Nation, almost, if not quite, unique in our New Jersey municipal experience. Of course his opportunity for public service has in large degree been a by-product of his headship of this Bell unit, but that emphasizes rather than detracts from his community value. He has reflected honor on his business organization without impairing his efficiency, and unless there is some obstacle in the considerations which properly prevail in a nationwide system of Bell magnitude, it seems appropriate and usual to recognize this outstanding man in the manner the Directors would like. I know that he would not assent without your approval, and we would not want to insist upon our suggestion if directly or indirectly objectionable to the parent organization.

I am hopeful that there may be no objection to establishing the permanent memorial we contemplate.

With high personal regard, I am,

Yours very truly,
John R. Hardin

There were, however, tragedies and disappointments in Chester I. Barnard's life. His only child, a daughter, Frances died in childbirth in 1951. Her untimely death had a deep and lasting effect. As one close to him observed, "Barnard lost some of his vitality." Frances had been very close to her father and had inherited his intellect and graciousness. At Smith College she had been a top student and active participant in school activities. She died leaving three children whom Mrs. Barnard and her husband tried to help through their teens.

Barnard wrote his daughter a long letter on economics which was later printed privately. It was a response to questions Frances had raised about her studies. In it Barnard reveals a clear understanding of marginal productivity theory and a warmth and sense of humor seldom found in his other writings.[60]

Another disappointment, but one which is difficult to assess, was the reaction of his contemporaries at New Jersey Bell. Several of the old-timers who had served in his organization were only lukewarm in describing his administration, for example, one of them observed, "He was really a good staff man rather than a line executive." Kenneth R. Andrews points out in the introduction to the thirtieth anniversary printing of *The Functions,* "His associates and successors in the Bell System have not made him a corporate or folk hero, those I have known do not find occasion to speak of him at all."[61]

Within New Jersey Bell Barnard had a number of critics who suggested that under his leadership the introduction of dial service had proceeded too slowly. World War II, with its sudden increase in demand for dial service, had precipitated some of the criticisms. That Barnard was well aware of this is indicated by a paper he wrote and distributed within the New Jersey Bell System.[62] This paper appears to be Barnard's defense of his administration through a summary of the history of the dial program in New Jersey. He stated that New Jersey would have complete dial service around the mid-1950s. He continued,

> These facts give occasion for inquiry as to why dial service has not been developed more extensively in New Jersey prior to this time. It seems that many in our organization have not been sufficiently informed of the factors that have controlled decisions in this field. . . . It therefore seems important to prepare this memorandum for the use of many in our organization whose regular work does not so easily permit them to be informed on this subject. . . .

No judgment of the issue is, or can be, attempted here. This episode is included for three reasons: first, because there was, and is, some doubt on the part of Barnard's contemporaries and colleagues in industry regarding the success of his telephone career, and, second, because it is apparent that Barnard was aware of these doubts. This episode is also included because it gives rise to a broader question, the answer to which has been sought by

---

[60]Chester I. Barnard, "Concerning the Modern Price System and Related Matters."

[61]Chester I. Barnard, *The Functions of the Executive,* 30th anniversary ed., intro., by Kenneth R. Andrews (Cambridge: Harvard University Press, 1968), p. ix. All other references to *The Functions* are to the first edition and its reprintings.

[62]Chester I. Barnard, *The History and Economics of the Dial Program of the New Jersey Bell Telephone Company* (Newark: New Jersey Bell, 1947).

many and is still to be obtained: The question was aptly phrased by a colleague of Barnard's, "To what degree can a philosopher-king be a good king?"[63]

---

[63]Letter from J. R. Pierce, director of research at Bell Telephone Laboratories in Murray Hill, New Jersey, October 16, 1961, to Peter J. Cabrera.

III.

Barnard's Philosophy and Thought Processes

If one understands Barnard's habit of mind or general thought process, his works are more readily understood. The purpose of this chapter is to provide such a framework. What follows deals with Barnard's humanism, his empiricism, his speculative philosophy, and his framework for analysis.

Barnard's Humanism

Central to understanding Barnard's life and thoughts is his humanistic position. He attached primary importance to man and to the development of man's faculties, affairs, and well-being. In fact, a cornerstone of Barnardian thinking is to respect each individual as a distinctive human being: "You have to distinguish between ability and its compensation and the *work of people as individuals.*" To illustrate this Barnard told the story of his father:

> My father was one of the finest men I have even known in life. He also had imagination, but he did not have either education or the natural ability to be a real manager of anything. He was a little bit too tender-hearted. If he were selling eggs at 13½ cents a dozen and a boy came, he always gave them for 13 cents instead of 14 cents. I respected him as much as anybody I have ever met and known intimately. I don't think he was an able person. That *is the the distinction we should always keep in mind in dealing with people from whatever level to whatever level, to have people know that we* really consider them as our equals . . . who command respect as much as anybody else.[1]

The focus of Barnard's humanistic position is his treatment of the individual. At various times he reiterated the theme that respect for the dignity and worth of the individual is a primary consideration. In 1935 he gave a talk at Princeton University in which he succinctly summarized his position: "I believe that progress in personnel relations involves recog-

---

[1]From a talk to employees of New Jersey Bell Telephone, as quoted in the *Newark Sunday News,* March 28, 1948. Emphasis added.

nition that the development of the individual employee is of first importance."[2] Closely related to his concern for the individual was Barnard's position relative to political democracy. In a December 6, 1946 letter to Herbert Simon he compares his attitude toward political democracy with Simon's: "I probably give a somewhat higher value to political democracy than you . . . because I think the exercise of political democracy adds something to the dignity of the individual, or should do so."

His concern for the individual involved recognition of the conflicting forces encountered in the lives of men. Barnard's approach was to seek "a proper balance." He attempted to integrate differences and avoid extremes. This theme and his values regarding what men ought to seek are found in an unpublished commencement address titled "What Other Purpose?" which he gave at the Polytechnic Institute of Brooklyn on June 17, 1936.

> . . . One thing only would I distill from the thoughts of men concerning the art of life. This is that the use of all our faculties in proper balance, the avoidance of extremes, and the subordination of immediate self-interest to the larger purpose of aid to others is the road leading to the great accomplishment. This achievement involves perpetual struggle. In the manifold nature of our being there are many ends and purposes between which we must secure a harmony and balance. It is this perpetual conflict of the moral being that gives us our great duties and opportunities. It is not to be healthy or strong animals, nor to boast wealth, nor to acquire individual glory, nor to rule men, nor to make of ourselves prophets to which we can aspire, nor to achieve, which would in the end grant satisfaction. To support ourselves and our families is our first duty to ourselves and to society as well; to contribute to the material welfare of mankind; to aid and support the political institutions of our time; to promote the art of cooperation among us without sacrificing our own sense of personal respect and responsibility; to hold fast to our own convictions without violence to those of others; to keep ourselves throughout loyal to our own code of right conduct, and to struggle upward toward the light of the Ideal and the Spirit — these as one harmonious whole should be the ends of our ambition, the never ending achievement of each day's work yet never attainable, the only course which promises enduring satisfaction.

This quote presents a number of ideas that are found in Barnard's theory of organization and management, for example, that the executive needs to maintain a proper balance between a variety of ends and purposes; that

---

[2]Chester I. Barnard, "Some Principles and Basic Considerations in Personnel Relations" (Address to the Fifth Summer Conference Course in Industrial Relations, Graduate College, Princeton University, September 20, 1935), as reprinted in *Organization and Management,* p. 23.

the executive needs to resolve the perpetual moral crises which he faces, to be morally creative; that responsibility is a critical aspect of effectiveness.

Barnard's personal philosophy is further revealed in a speech he made on June 14, 1932, upon being presented a "distinguished service medallion" for services rendered to the city of Newark. In receiving this award from the Newark Exchange Club he said:

> . . . to me, as to most men who have reflected on life and society, popularity, indicating so often mere accommodation to the sentiment of the moment, seems to be only tinsel — a bauble that is an unworthy ambition and a dangerous one. Who knows how often the love of acclaim warps the judgment and undermines the principles of men? Though the power that popularity sometimes gives must not be deprecated because it must be applied usefully to the highest purposes, the abiding esteem, the high respect, the enduring influence that make for true progress can come, it seems to me, only from a personal service — a service which expresses a worthy ambition, which reveals an ability given by devotion to a high cause; a service possible only with the perspective that grows as selfishness diminishes; a service which demands the fortitude that arises from adherence to principle.
>
> The significance of this occasion is, I think, that you say to this community that the esteem and respect of one's fellow citizens for civic and community service is a thing to be valued; and that to win it is worth emulating. What people will do depends so much upon their point of view, their philosophy, their faith concerning what is worthwhile; and these things are determined so much by precept and by example. This is why, rather than for reasons of courtesy or personal gratification, I lend myself so conspicuously to this ceremony.
>
> For some time now, we have let ourselves become indoctrinated with the belief that the important things are to get money, to impress one's neighbors by possessions, to acquire shallow power, to secure notoriety, to place pleasure above character, to make of one's self the center of the universe. It seems to me high time to teach the truth and preach the faith. Man cannot live by prosperity alone. Sweat and brain are but the tools of a process that must be guided to a goal that is beyond self, not within self. The cooperation that is essential to our mere survival must come from the spirit; it cannot come from a brute selfishness that measures success in power to destroy; that mistakes cunning for intellect; that confuses daring speculation for courage; that calls leadership that which only leads astray; that mistakes manners for culture and clothes for character. The cooperation that now and henceforth is necessary to repel the tide of barbarism that is welling up within us means more than mere acquiescence in democracy, more than a mere accommodation to the interferences of the crowd. It means genuine restraint of self in many directions, it means actual service for no reward, it

means courage to fight for principles rather than for things, it means genuine subjection of destructive personal interest to social interests.[3]

This 1932 talk foreshadows a number of concepts which appear in Barnard's later works. Of central importance is that "ultimately cooperation must come from the spirit" and the recognition of limitation of financial and material incentives. In fact, Barnard's final chapter in *The Functions* concludes that "out of the void comes the spirit that shapes the ends of men."[4]

Barnard's Empiricism

As a humanist Barnard advocated service to society, personal initiative, and integrity. He had faith in the superior faculties of mankind and saw the purpose of individuals to be contributing to the society as a whole within a framework of individual freedom and responsibility. Barnard was almost an idealistic humanist concerned with both the dignity and worth of the individual and the general welfare of society. There is yet another perspective for viewing Barnard: he was an empiricist; the practical realist whom John Foster Dulles sought out in order to help a group of theologians "keep their feet on the ground." Barnard's empiricism, that is his dependence on experience and observation and his distrust of "science," appear in numerous places in his writing. With respect to his own intellectual development Barnard felt he learned most from experience. In his unpublished notes he states, "So far as I am definitely aware, the notions here expressed arise chiefly from reflection upon experience; but I suspect this cannot be true. . . ."

Despite his belief in learning by experience, Barnard did on several occasions list books that had been useful to him in writing "Some Obscure Aspects of Human Relations" and *The Functions of the Executive*.[5] Almost

---

[3]Unpublished notes of address to Newark Exchange Club, June 14, 1932, p. 2.

[4]*The Functions*, p. 284.

[5]The books Barnard listed in his unpublished notes as being useful in writing "Some Obscure Aspects of Human Relations," an unpublished address delivered to the New Jersey State Chamber of Commerce, Jan. 7, 1937, were Alfred Korzbski, *Science and Sanity: An Introduction to Non-Aristotelian Systems and General Semantics* (New York: Science Press, 1961); C. K. Ogden and I. A. Richards, *The Meaning of Meaning* (New York: Routledge, 1936); Arthur F. Bentley, *Behavior, Knowledge, Fact* (Bloomingdale, Ind.: The Principia Press, 1935); and Alfred North Whitehead, *Process and Reality: An Essay in Cosmology* (New York: Macmillan, 1936).

With respect to *The Functions of the Executive*, Barnard named five works which "as a whole seem to give a general background of scientific thought that lead ultimately to a sense of organization in general harmony [with Barnard's concepts]. . . ." They were Eugene Ehrlick, *The Fundamental Principles of Sociology of Law*, trans. by W. L. Moll (New York: Russell & Russell, 1936); Vilfredo Pareto, *Mind and Society* (New York: Harcourt Brace, 1935); John R. Commons, *Institutional Economics* (New York: Macmillan, 1934); J. F. Brown, *Psychology and the Social Order* (New York: McGraw Hill,

all of these books emphasize the difficulty or inability of social science in dealing with the complex causality found in the subject. Barnard summarized the difficulty in a talk given in 1947.

> Some years ago I first became dimly aware of radical differences in ways of thinking as between two kinds of situations; one, where simple cause and effect or what I now call linear reasoning is sufficient and effective; and, two, the reasoning applicable to systems consisting of a number of interdependent variables. Pareto in his *Mind and Society* discusses this subject, saying that the only logic applicable to systems of many interdependent variables is that of sets of differential equations. There is no purely verbal description of such systems that can be adequate. Nevertheless, it is not possible to apply mathematics to the description of such systems unless the variable elements composing them can be measured and this is rarely the case. Consequently, the understanding of such systems has to be a matter of judgment almost aesthetic in character and this feeling for the situation to the extent it is attempted to be expressed in words has to be translated into simple cause and effect reasoning or into terms of strategic factors. Such translation is always defective, frequently misleading and not too seldom completely erroneous in practical consequence. It involves the error of misplaced concreteness, to use Whitehead's term, or the fallacy of "other things being equal."

> Now, the fact is that in varying degrees those concerned in the management of business enterprises, or indeed of other kinds of organized activities are almost always concerned with judgments about changes in systems involving numerous interdependent variables. In most cases they cannot measure the factors with which they are concerned and they are unable to express accurately their sense of the changes in com-

---

1936); and Kurt Koffka, *Principles of Gestalt Psychology* (New York: Harcourt Brace, 1935).

Regarding these Barnard stated in an unpublished draft of *The Functions*, p. 13:

> These books as a group serve to strip off obsessions and presuppositions that prevent an open approach. Each departs from traditional and historical views, and marks a beginning of new attacks on their fields. Each of them presents a good deal that is original or of recent origin. This novelty is not, however, their merit, which consists of reasoned support of theories of aspects of human life that closely reflect important sectors of the world at least as it appears to me. . . .
> Though I have not placed it in the above list because it is of the utmost generality, the most important idealogical basis for the theory of organization is Whitehead's *Process and Reality*. This is a profound work in speculative philosophy and metaphysics which presents a fundamental organic philosophy of the universe and of reality. The theory of organization here presented was not derived from it but from experience, but it conforms to Whitehead's treatise at least analogically. Moreover, if his philosophy be accepted, a sound theory of organization would, as I believe this one does, conform to it.

binations resulting from specific action to modify one or another of the variables. It is to this state of affairs that I think is to be ascribed the confusion and indeed the numerous contradictions in the statements of businessmen and others about what they are doing or proposing; in fact, the techniques for dealing with systems of more than a few interdependent variables, according to my friend, Dr. Warren Weaver, await development. At the lower end of the spectrum where we are dealing with a small number of interdependent and independent variables, the techniques are highly developed and accurate. At the other end where we are dealing with large statistical aggregates, the techniques have also been highly developed. But for the intermediate range, systems of say 5 to 50 to 100 variables, the techniques are not adequate. The new mathematical computing machines may help in this field.[6]

Thus, Barnard's empiricism was based upon the observation that science has limits. Accordingly, in discussions of development of executives he deemphasized intellectual ability and academic training and emphasized intuition, know-how, hunches, and similar characteristics which are usually related to intensive experiences. Similarly he emphasized the use of precept and example in training executives and the inculcation of attitudes within organizations.

It was his realism and practical nature, his ability to free himself from conventional myths, which led to his significant contributions such as the recognition of the role of the informal organization, the importance of acceptance to the use of authority, the role of nonlogical thought processes, the concept of complex casuality in organizational settings, the communication function and process, the limits of material incentives in motivating men, the limits and methods of decision making, the dispersive tendencies of individuals, the complexity and instability of motives, and the never-ending burden of decisions. These were relatively startling concepts when he first presented them and many still find them difficult to accept. They are, however, concepts which describe reality; concepts which practitioners know to be sound.

The following excerpts from Barnard's papers illustrate his concern for "what is," his empirical nature, and his recognition of the complexity of social phenomena.

In a letter written to John Romanition of Irvington, New Jersey, on June 8, 1937, Barnard stated:

I suppose it takes a certain, and perhaps an unusual, course of experience, and a somewhat philosophic trend of mind to make sense of the

---

[6]Chester I. Barnard, "Some Aspects of Organization Relevant to Industrial Research," in *The Conditions of Industrial Progress: Twenty-Fifth Anniversary of the Industrial Research Department* (Philadelphia: Wharton School of Finance and Commerce, University of Pennsylvania, 1947) pp. 68–69.

THE BASIC BARNARD

contradictions and confusions of life. Most people most of the time seem
to get along pretty well by disregarding the contradictions, and by
assuming for the time being that many things are true which are not.
I have learned to recognize that many of the things which appear to
be contradictions really are not, but that some degree of confusion,
conflict and difference of opinion and interest is naturally and inherently necessary. I suppose it all goes back to the fact that the physical
conditions under which we live are very far from stable.

In the unpublished notes for his 1937 lecture, "Some Obscure Aspects of
Human Relations," Barnard states:

That which is most pertinent to this lecture, however, is not what men
of affairs talk about or how they talk, but that what they say seems so
often to be in conflict with what they do. They often express convictions denied by their action. Self-contradiction seems to the detached
and critical observer a most characteristic aspect of the behavior of
reputable and respected men of affairs.

In a similar vein Barnard told a meeting of the American Society of
Mechanical Engineers that:

Through a period of years, as a matter of interest, I have endeavored,
without any success, to find out what the intellectual processes were
and what we can possibly mean by "intuition." My initial interest in
the subject was quite practical. Without casting any aspersions, it was
an interest in discovering why it is that people who had scientific training so frequently had no sense.

I concluded as I had considered the subject thoroughly and thought
about it and observed people, that one of the important limitations
of our civilization has been the over-emphasis, the inclusive emphasis,
of the importance of the logical processes, and the sciences which have
developed out of them, and the exclusion of the appreciation of the
other faculties. . . .

It is possible as you know, from art, literature and other things, to
increase the non-logical or intuitive expertness of behavior by conditioning. People learn to feel things by working in them and by working with people who are adept in handling them.[7]

Barnard was an empiricist who readily admitted that life is complex and
man faces inherent conflict in both his organizations and broader society.
He recognized that the problems of man in society are not readily soluble.
With humanistic faith, however, he emphasized that one must not main-

[7] From notes in Barnard's papers on a 1942 talk given on inventiveness and ingenuity
at the 1942 Annual Meeting of the American Society of Mechanical Engineers.

tain a defeatist attitude. This general philosophy is illustrated in a letter written to William F. Whyte on August 28, 1946:

> In connection with my work in the atomic bomb area I have had occasion several times to emphasize a distinction between pessimism and defeatism. I have been extremely pessimistic about the possibilities of the international control of atomic energy production and have emphasized that a very thoroughgoing pessimism was almost essential to the development of the possibility of control. On the other hand, I cannot accept the defeatist position because I have more than once seen occur what seemed impossible. That, in fact, occurred in connection with the State Department report on control. It seemed to me at first impossible that we could agree on such a report, extremely unlikely that a report would be accepted if written, and even more unlikely that Mr. Baruch would adopt it — but these things all happened.

> It seems to me extremely unlikely that human beings can control the evolution of their society. This does not mean that what men deliberately do will not affect that evolution, but that the effects will be different than desired and many effects will be completely unforeseen. Is it not evident that we have very little understanding of complex social phenomena even after occurrence?

Barnard reiterated the belief that although one cannot see the solution to a difficult situation he should not give up hope. In a discussion of the control of atomic energy he stated:

> Well, the first thing to say is that you must not get hopeless about the inability to see the solution of a difficult situation. Let me give you an example. This is after the fact. The Social Science Research Council a year or two ago got a group of fellows to do a job on historiography and they decided to take Civil War histories as a good field to work in. As I recall it, they found there were many Civil War histories and there were some of them in the class known as single cause. There was one cause only for the war. The difficulty is that histories differed as to which was the cause. Then there was another group called multi-cause histories; the thing didn't depend upon just one cause. It was a great complex of two, three, four, five or ten things; and there were a number of histories written of that kind. Unfortunately they did not agree as to what were the multi-causes that were involved. And others were non-causal histories that did not find any cause of the war. It was just one of those things. But my point is that you can look back to the Revolutionary War in this country. After it is all over, and you have read all the history, you still do not see how this nation could have worked out its destiny, but it did. . . .

We do not see the solution of the future. But we have to be prepared to make the sacrifices that facilitate a solution that we cannot see.[8]

Barnard's Speculative Philosophy

Closely related to his empiricism is the development of Barnard's speculative philosophy. As used here the term speculative philosophy means "the endeavor to frame a coherent, logical, necessary system of general ideas in terms of which every element of our experience can be interpreted."[9] Barnard sought to develop such a framework of concepts and constructs which would guide practical thought and action. As he stated in a talk in 1935:

> . . . I am sure that a consideration of general purposes, "principles," and underlying conceptions — what we may call the philosophic approach to the concrete problems — is intensely practical. Indeed, it is almost necessary that we unite in such an approach in order that our consideration of the specific problems may be intelligent, and that our discussion of them may be intelligible. . . . Not infrequently our failures in this respect permit us to do well what had best not be done at all, or to do badly or omit what may be essential.[10]

Barnard's major contribution to speculative philosophy is *The Functions of the Executive*. The philosophy of organization which he developed has been popularized as "open-system theory," which means that social phenomena occur in systems which are part of broader systems. The complexity of each such system limits our understanding of cause and effect. The parts of the system are related; they interact and are at the same time determined and determining forces in the system. The characteristics of any specific part tend to determine the nature of the system, but at the same time the nature of the system tends to determine the characteristics of that specific part.

Thus, a central concept underlying Barnard's reasoning about organization is that of system theory and all of the corollaries of system theory tend to appear within his comments about organization. Some consistent themes in Barnard's work are the limits of simple cause-and-effect reasoning in solving problems; the whole is more than the sum of its parts; to change one part is to change the interactions and, thus, to change the system as a whole.

---

[8]Chester I. Barnard, "The Proposals for an International Authority to Control Atomic Energy: Great Issues Course," *Dartmouth Alumni Magazine*, February 1948, p. 36.

[9]Whitehead, *Process and Reality*, p. 1.

[10]"Some Principles and Basic Considerations in Personnel Relations" in *Organization and Management*, p. 3.

54

Similarly Barnard sees organizations, as well as persons, as systems seeking balance. (What modern organization theorists identify as a "steady state.") The system adjusts to internal and external forces to maintain a dynamic equilibrium. This balance is constantly changing so that the interaction of the forces which bring it about is usually different from time to time. The equilibrium itself is not a constant point or focus for balance. It is more like a balloon floating in air than the fulcrum of a teeter-totter or lever.

Barnard's entire theory of organization is best viewed as a special application of open-system theory. His treatment centers on a description of the nature of organizations as open systems, involving consideration of the parts and elements which make up the system, for example, individuals and the broader environmental factors. It also involves such processes of functioning systems as communication, decisions, feedback, identifying purpose, motivation, and incentive. Thus, Barnard states that executive functions cannot be segregated from the functioning organization because they are parts of the organization as a whole. Carrying out executive functions involves a sense of the organization as a whole as well as of the total situation relevant to it.[11]

Barnard's Framework of Analysis

To understand Barnard's writings one should recognize his open-system approach. Within it a critical aspect of Barnard's thinking is his use of polarity to refine analysis. Generally in dealing with a subject Barnard seeks the extreme positions and then attempts to arrive at a balanced point of view.

His major work is dominated by dichotomies, of central importance is his concern for individualism and collectivism. In 1934 he discussed his view of this conflict at the Fourth Annual Economic Conference for Engineers:

> Over twenty-five years ago, I finished my work as a university student saturated with the conception that the individual was almost the sole factor in human progress and that systematized group activities, organization, cooperation, collectivism were quite secondary, or of incidental importance. This conception was natural and quite logical in view of my experience up to that time.
>
> In the first place, I had been taught by the reiteration of precept that individual initiative, individual effort, individual thrift, individual ambition, individual character, were the main elements of civilized life and progress. In those days the chief emphasis was still placed upon

---

[11]*The Functions*, p. 235.

individualism in education, in economics and in politics, to the relative neglect of the facts and the problems of cooperation, organization and collective effort.

Moreover, having been thrown on my own resources at an early date, I had acquired chiefly by means of my own efforts both a secondary school and a college education, in the process of which I selected for myself the institutions which I attended, learned several methods of livelihood and undertook all of the business and other arrangements necessary to conduct my affairs independently. Consequently, I regarded myself in relation to the world in which I lived much as many farmers see their relationship to their harvests — the energy of the sun, the chemistry of the soil, the vital but undefinable processes of life, which really make the corn grow, are accepted as part of the universal gift of nature, and the farmer may — and from some points of view must — attribute to his own energy and knowledge the harvest that he gathers, even though in fact his efforts are quite superficial and incidental to natural processes that really produce it. Somewhat similarly I looked upon the family, the social groups of which I was a part, the schools and universities, the railroads, the organizations of industry, the government, as things made available to me by nature rather than by the deliberate and largely conscious effort of men acting in cooperation.

In this state of mind, I obtained employment in one of the greatest and most complex collective enterprises ever organized on a commercial basis — the Bell Telephone System. Its large capital was collectively supplied by hundreds of thousands of investors, its operations required the employment of hundreds of thousands of persons, its management was carried on by thousands carefully arranged in a hierarchy of positions and authorities; its legal existence was authorized by a collectivity called the State, and its conduct, its rights, its privileges were governed not only by an immense body of general law and custom, derived from collective action through many generations, but also by specific statutes and regulatory authorities similarly evolved and created by society for the regulation of the business. Even the service itself depended upon a collective social condition so that it was not possible in general to sell to any individual the services unless many other individuals also were subscribers to it.

I quickly learned that all of this collective operation, both within and without the organization, possessed tremendous power which transcended the sum of the efforts of the individuals directly concerned in it, and that it also accomplished many things impossible except by cooperation on a grand scale.

These facts obviously were back of the constantly expressed phrases — "The good of the organization," "The service as a whole" — which seemed to be the real basis for what I at first felt to be repression of the individual who was becoming less and less significant. This repression was evident not so much in specific directions concerning work to be done as by the inhibitions and prohibitions arising out of the intangible barriers of departments, grades and ranks, policies, appropriations, laws, prejudices and economic limitations of consumers—so that I soon experienced a reaction away from the rugged individualism — with which I entered the service, toward the conception that facts and principles and organizations and collective action were everything, and the individual was and could be nothing.

Such a conception of the world in which I had begun to work was, I think, as destructive as that of extreme individualism for, since, I could not eliminate myself from myself — since my supervisors continued to regard me as an individual — since society continued to treat me for better or worse as an individual — I was in danger either of falling into a complete lethargy from my inability to reconcile two apparently contradictory states of affairs or of attempting to treat myself either as a slightly conscious and unimportant cog in a gigantic machine, or as an anarchist determined to assert my individuality in destructive action. You can see all about you men and women whose escape from the dilemma due to existence of individual life and the university of collective society has been through one of the three doors I have described. In the language of social welfare work they are "maladjusted."

Due perhaps principally to the intelligence and patience of the supervisors under whose direction I had the good fortune to be placed, I happily escaped from the dilemma through the fourth door which was that of directing my individual efforts not only in conformance with, but in furtherance of the objectives of the organization. I then gradually learned that properly understood and with intelligent adjustment the individual can secure from collective organization great expansion of individual opportunity for accomplishment and for self-expression. Nevertheless, week after week there constantly arose and there still arise, the dilemmas which perhaps are best expressed as the conflict between one's duty to one's self and one's duty to the ever present collectivities of which one is inescapably a part.

I did not in the early days recognize the problem as a universal one. I at first thought that it was more or less a peculiarity of my own position or of the particular organization to which I was attached; and I did not regard the problem philosophically until I subsequently found myself in responsible though minor positions of management in which it was necessary for me consciously to determine in a limited degree how to solve this problem not for myself but both for an organization and for the individuals who composed it. Such experience, the World

War with its tremendous cooperation and regimentation of people, and
finally reflections on the state of affairs of recent years have made me
understand that one and perhaps the most vital of all problems of
human life is how effectively to harmonize two principles of life which
in isolation seem to be utterly opposed — the one systematic arrangements of human affairs, cooperation, organization, regimentation, collectivity; and the other the dynamic individual.[12]

The dichotomy of the individual and the organization is a critical concept that permeates Barnard's work. To understand it one should recognize
that to Barnard each individual is a distinctive, unique human being. Each
person learns in a variety of ways, but most important is the fact that he
is frequently not fully aware of his own thought processes, values, or
actions. To Barnard, thus, the individual often does not understand himself;
his behavior is influenced by personal needs and emotions of which he is
probably not consciously aware, he tends to rationalize rather than to
behave rationally, he functions on intuition, hunch, and the know-how
which develops from intensive experiences. Moreover, his behavior is frequently reflexive, responsive, and autonomic. In essence then, Barnard
sees much of the individual's behavior as occurring at a subconscious level
and as based on a logic outside of the individual's awareness. The adjec-
tives associated with the individual's behavior and thoughts are subjective,
emotional, nonlogical, intuitive, personal.

In contrast Barnard sees formal organizations as rational structures.
Their logic is communicated to individuals. Thus, formal organizations
are dominated by stated goals or ends, are impersonal, arrive at ends by
logical processes, delegate various tasks to individuals, and develop specialization. In summary, formal organizations tend to be planned, rational,
logical, and impersonal.

It is with these underlying assumptions that Barnard analyzes dimensions of formal organizations. Although his entire speculative philosophy
is discussed in the following chapters, it may help to highlight some of
Barnard's dichotomies. For convenience we can redefine the basic or
fundamental polarity as personal and impersonal, where personal refers
to the individual and his needs and impersonal refers to the organization
and its management. Following are a number of the dipoles which Barnard
established.

---

[12]Chester I. Barnard, "Collectivism and Individualism in Industrial Management"
(Address delivered at the Fourth Annual Economic Conference for Engineers, Stevens
Engineering Camp, Johnsonburg, N. J., August 11, 1934, pp. 2–6) was published from
stenographic notes in *The New Jersey Bell* 7 (1934) and was reprinted as a pamphlet
in 1937.

PHILOSOPHY AND THOUGHT PROCESSES

Personal	*Impersonal*
nonlogical thought processes	logical thought processes
informal organization	formal organization
responsive behavior	decisive behavior
efficiency	effectiveness
free will	determinism
moral responsibilities	legal responsibilities
authority based upon consent	authority based upon hierarchial position
subjective interpretation of an order	objective character of an order
decisions as to ends (concerned with moral questions), thus subjective and personal	decisions as to means (concerned with technical issues), thus objective and relatively impersonal

Conclusion

Barnard's stated humanism is consistent with his own behavior, as a study of his life indicates. Furthermore, his practical, pragmatic approach to the concrete problems of organization dominated his conceptualization. He judged men by what they did rather than what they said. He emphasized experience, precept, and example and distrusted reliance on intellectual training for developing skilled men of affairs or executives.

Most importantly, he developed his speculative philosophy to help understand and order what he experienced. In a May 11, 1945, letter to Herbert Simon he observed the importance of his arm chair philosophizing. "It is a necessary process in the achievement of concepts. As A. N. Whitehead has in effect well said, it is impossible to get anywhere with bare facts without a theory since without a theory there is no basis for determining what facts are relevant and evidential."

Barnard's speculative philosophy was anchored in open-system theory and his approach was to frame issues in terms of opposites (dipoles or pairs). Underlying much of his analysis is the basic dichotomy of the individual and the organization. On the one side he deals with emotions, subjective data, subconscious behavior, on the other with rational, impersonal, objective management. As a humanist Barnard sought a balanced point of view, that is, a way to benefit both the individual and mankind. The following chapters bring together the essential features of Barnard's speculative philosophy.

59

IV.

Concept of Formal Organization

The preceding sections dealt with Barnard's background and theoretical orientation. We now consider his concepts of organization and the elements of organization. This chapter focuses on Barnard's definition and description of formal organization and the next considers special processes and aspects of formal organization. Together these two chapters summarize the essence of Barnard's theory of formal organization.

Barnard's Goals in Writing The Functions of the Executive

To understand what a man has said it is helpful to know what motivates him to say it. This statement is especially true in the case of Chester I. Barnard. Why should a practicing business executive write a book or give a series of lectures that are highly abstract and extremely difficult for most people to comprehend? The answer to this question lies in the state of the art of management at the time that Barnard wrote. When he began to prepare his Lowell Institute Lectures he intended simply to describe what executives do and how they work. He soon discovered that this could be done only by relating the executive's functions to the structure and dynamic characteristics of organizations. In turning his attention to management and organization Barnard discovered that the literature suffered from "vagueness, ambiguity, and non-standard nomenclature."[1] Hence at the outset Barnard had to define his terms and otherwise carefully explain the meaning he gave to words. Probably more important was the fact that not only were the terms used ambiguous, but the concepts were extremely vague. "Thus, the exposition depended upon the selection and construction of concepts that would permit of a logically consistent treatment of the subject matter with the maximum of definiteness and the minimum of ambiguity. Scientific communication in this field awaits the development and acceptance of a set of concepts and a definite language."[2]

---

[1] *Organization and Management*, p. 112.
[2] *Ibid.*, p. 112.

Barnard's central goal was to provide sound generalizations about social cooperation which could provide an adequate theoretical basis for training in the administrative professions. *The Functions* was written to develop concepts and ideas that would provide the framework of a theory of organization and management. As Barnard said: "It is necessary to have such a framework to get 'basing points,' as it were, some place to start getting order out of bewildering chaos and to have enough rigidity — consistency — to keep things in order long enough at least to consider them."[3]

In summary, we see that Barnard was attempting to write a general theoretical work (that is, a speculative philosophy) which would have wide applicability. The state of the field of knowledge in which he was writing required him to forge his own tools. The goal which he sought, a generalized statement, required a high level of discourse; he could not deal with concrete phenomena without becoming bogged down in detail and losing the possibility of wide applicability. Thus, he was concerned with the "broadest generalizations rigorously defined, logically consistent and non-contradictory. . . ."[4]

His theory of organization deals with the broader environmental setting in which organization functions, the definition of "organization," the nature of individuals, and informal organization.[5]

The Nature of Organization

In a parable a wise man asks: "What is the essential ingredient if one is to wash an elephant?" The answer is that one must have an elephant. Similarly if one is to manage he must have an organization. The functions of the executive are performed in organizations and can be understood only in the context of organization. Hence, the starting place for discussing executive functions is the theory of organization.

It is easier to describe than to define an organization. As the term is commonly used it refers to such things as churches, schools, business firms, hospitals, and so forth. One of the problems in defining organization is that for analysis it is necessary to have a description that has general applicability. The goal is to generalize and be able to discuss the broad spectrum of organizations in terms of their common features; yet, the tendency is to think in terms of specifics. For example, when a person talks of organi-

---

[3]*Ibid.*, p. 131.

[4]*Ibid.*, p. 126.

[5]The reader should recognize that the materials presented here are an interpretation of what Barnard said. His discourse has been summarized and clarified rather than precisely translated.

zation he is usually referring to a specific organization with unique characteristics related to buildings, persons, geographic location, and so forth.

The need to define organization in terms of common elements guided Barnard's thinking. It is not that the unique features of a specific organization are not important, rather that the first step in developing a theory of organization is to define the phenomenon in a manner that is meaningful and allows generalization.[6]

The definition of the term "organization" used by Barnard is designed to meet his goal. He noted, however, that one must differentiate between formal and informal organizations. While these two are intimately related and formal organization cannot exist for long without informal, Barnard built his definition around the concept of formal organization.

Barnard defines a formal organization as a *"system of consciously coordinated activities of two or more persons."*[7]

By careful analysis of this definition we can derive an understanding of much of Barnard's thinking. For example, Barnard identifies formal organization as a system. In a sense this use is analogous to the use of field of gravity or electromagnetic field in the physical sciences. They are defined in terms of their effects. For example:

> . . . an electromagnet when actuated by an electric current is said to create an electromagnetic field, the existence of which is only known by phenomena which result when certain other things are put within that field. But none of these objective things are the field, nor is the electric current the electromagnetic force, though it is or carries the electromotive energy essential to it.

> Similarly, persons are the objective sources of the organization forces which occupy the organization field. These forces derive from energies that are found only in persons. They become organization forces only when certain conditions obtain within the field, and are evidenced only by certain phenomena such as words and other action, or are inferred by concrete results imputed to such action. But neither the persons nor the objective results are themselves the organization. If they are treated

---

[6]Since this discussion is concerned with the common aspects of organizations, it is limited in its usefulness with respect to any specific organization, except that a study of common features allows us to arrive at general principles which may in turn help in understanding a particular organization. The study of organization involves a comprehension of the common aspects and then an ability to differentiate among organizations and to understand each specific one as a unique cooperative system. For development of this view see William B. Wolf, "Organization Constructs: A Guide to Understanding Organizations," *Journal of the Academy of Management* 1 (April 1958): 7–15, and William B. Wolf, ed., *Management: Readings Toward a General Theory* (Belmont, Calif.: Wadsworth, 1964).

[7]*The Functions,* p. 73. Emphasis in original.

as if they were, inconsistencies and inadequacies of explanation of phenomena ensue.[8]

Thus, to Barnard it was essential to focus upon organization as "an integrated aggregate of actions and interactions having a continuity in time."[9] He rejected the concept of organization as a definite group of people coordinated to achieve a goal or goals.[10] Instead his definition embraced actions contributing to the purpose of organization. It included investors, customers, clients, and suppliers.

Once Barnard's definition is clearly understood his treatment of formal organization follows logically. For example, he says that an organization is a system of consciously coordinated activities or forces of two or more persons. From this one can infer that the properties of systems in general are applicable. Formal organization is, thus, more than the sum of its parts. One cannot reify formal organization by fractionating it and then simply adding its parts.

The basic concept of system involves field or gestalt theory. It is not new and in fact has been illustrated for thousands of years by the old Buddhist parable regarding the blind men and the elephant in which one blind man felt a leg, another an ear, another the tusk, another the trunk. When asked to describe the animal, the man who felt the leg said it was like a tree trunk, another that it was a winnowing fan, another that it was like a stone, and another that it was similar to a snake. Each attempted to describe the whole elephant in terms of the part which he had touched. None of them described the elephant accurately; for, by dealing with the parts in isolation, they failed to comprehend the whole. They failed to see the interrelation of the parts and, hence, could not understand the elephant as a functioning organism.

In conceptualizing organizations as systems, Barnard raises several important points which need to be recognized. The first is that organizations are in reality only partial systems. It is impossible to isolate a complete, whole organization. Rather organizations are composed of various subunits which in themselves are organizations. In addition each organization is part of bigger and more complex organizations. The importance of this observation is that it highlights a problem encountered in the study of organizations as systems, namely, that systems must be treated as wholes. A failure to do so will warp or distort the relations of the interdependent variables. Moreover in a system the whole is more than the sum of its parts. When two or more elements are brought together the net result is more than the sum of the two, for there are also the relations. Similarly, in more

---

[8]*Ibid.*, p. 76.
[9]*Organization and Management,* p. 112.
[10]*Ibid.*

complex systems the interactions of the parts with each other and with the whole to which they belong makes the system more than the sum of the parts. As an old Buddhist parable states, "There is no such thing as two, for no two things can be conceived without their relationship, and this makes three. . . ."[11]

When an organization is viewed as a partial system existing in a broader complex, Barnard's concept can be stated by biological analogy:

> the activities contributed by the individual, following biological anal-ogy, are in my thinking like the protoplasm and the energies constantly working into and out from the cell. When a new enterprise is under-taken it begins with a small group who are the founders or incorpora-tors, or by an individual who gathers about him an initial small group. It then expands as an organization by the development of additional cells or groups interlocked, by the constant circulation of individuals (more strictly, their activities) between groups. The principal interlock-ing activity is communication. In this way we achieve the complex formal organizations, some of very large size, familiar to us all.[12]

Once we accept that organizations are partial systems that grow very much like cells and that they add new unit organizations and in the proc-ess develop complex organizations, four conclusions follow: (1) The limit of effectiveness in complex organizations is a function of communication. Communication between the parts and the whole is essential for coordina-tion. (2) In complex organizations the necessity for communication almost invariably results in the development of an executive organization which maintains communication within and outside the organization. (3) Within complex organizations members must live with contradictory forces (for example, conflict of loyalty between the unit or subordinate organization and the superior or complex organization of which it is a part). (4) The organic nature or wholeness of organization develops because actions of participants in organizations contribute to both the special working unit of organization and other organization systems. It is this overlap, or simul-taneous contribution to two organizations by a single act, that leads to an organic whole in the complex organization.

Moreover, from the above we have a background for understanding Barnard's development of his general theory of organization. For example, Barnard's definition specifies that an organization is a system of consciously coordinated activities of two or more people. Key ideas implied center on

---

[11]Christmas Humphreys, *Buddhism* (Harmondsworth, Eng.: Penguin, 1951), p. 16.
[12]Chester I. Barnard, "Some Aspects of Organization Relevant to Industrial Research," in *The Conditions of Industrial Progress: Twenty-Fifth Anniversary of the Industrial Research Department* (Philadelphia: Wharton School of Finance and Commerce, Uni-versity of Pennsylvania, 1947), p. 65.

people and their general nature; coordination and its essential requirement, communication; motivating people to contribute cooperative efforts; and importance of purpose. Willingness to cooperate cannot develop without an objective for cooperation, that is, purpose. Purpose, thus, is the coordinating and unifying principle of formal organization.

The above is a brief statement of certain fundamental ideas which underlie Barnard's theory of organization. The points to be emphasized are that Barnard was seeking a general definition of formal organization and that his definition includes such key concepts as "system," consciously coordinated activities of persons and purpose, and continuity of time. From these we can deduce the importance to his theory of organization of system theory, the role of communication, the importance of motivation, and the function of purpose. In short, given Barnard's definition of formal organization and his goal in devising this definition it follows that he explores certain topics as strategic aspects of organization.

The Broader Environment of Organization

Before considering the strategic aspects of organization Barnard makes a number of observations as to the role of physical, biological, and social forces in influencing the nature of organization. In an unpublished draft of Part One of *The Functions* he discusses the limitations and restrictions placed by environment upon organization:

> The pressures, restrictions, and limitations which come from outside the organization lie in the environment in which the organization exists. This environment is of two kinds — the natural, physical environment; and the social environment of people, of governments, religions, numerous other organizations, and innumerable individuals. The physical environment imposes certain fixed and unchangeable laws of physics and chemistry, and important variabilities in conditions — such as climate, earthquakes, floods, droughts, solar emanations, biological phenomena. Adaptation to conditions is required, control of them as a whole is impossible. And this adaptation calls for techniques, science, arts, which largely develop outside the organization, and have often been the results of accidental discoveries. Both the conditions of nature and the state of techniques of adaptation and civilization are persistent limitations. Excepting in the most narrow sense, the organization is governed by them. Many things desired to be done cannot be done — "the state of the art" does not permit. . . .

> * * * * *

> Of the social aspects of the environment, we are on the whole more conscious. Even here, however, so much do we "take for granted" that

except for some immediate restriction or infringement of this social world upon our organization, we hardly recognize how completely we are dominated. Government, taxes, laws, licenses, franchises, regulations, orders, prohibitions, privileges — the very existence of our organizations depend upon and are controlled by them. Again, other organizations, competing, hostile, cooperating, conditioning. Then institutions, customs, cycles, habits, that inhere in our society, restraining, directing, forbidding. Again, the social resources — education, public order, public health, nation protection, which condition organization — advantages when regarded as improvements over what has been — limitations when regarded from the point of view of what could be, especially is all, were moulded from the point of view of our own organizations. Included in this social environment is the economic interplay of individual and organized forces reflecting remote nature, furnishing what are more consciously observed as limitation — the narrow range of choice in what can be sold, of what can be bought, the dependence upon money and upon the stability of money, of credit, of employment, and upon numerous details of economic life.

Because all other organizations, and even more all individuals, are closely held by these conditions of environment, we forget them, take them as part of the natural order and are aware only of a few irritations, stimuli, points of attack. But to the executive they are generally more evident than to others. . . .

. . . but to the executive the limitations and restrictions of the environment are thereby increased by the limitations found within the organization itself. For it is evident that the executive's work is almost completely that of developing, directing, managing, energizing organization. . . .

The limitations and restrictions encountered within organizations are partly ascribable to the biology of human beings. They are partly a reflection of the environment as it conditions individuals and they are partly inherent in organization itself — something more than can be ascribed merely or least directly to the natural and acquired limitations of individuals.

* * * * *

. . . At every turn, therefore, the executive is confronted, both as respects the environment of the organization and its internal constitution, with requirements, prohibitions, limitations, disabilities, inertia, obstruction, recalcitrance, disintegrating influences, that rule out one after another the possibilities and desirabilities as "impracticable," "not susceptible of accomplishment"; and that restrict the choice of the methods by which only the meagre remainder of "promising" ideas may be carried out.[13]

---

[13]Unpublished draft of Part One of *The Functions*, pp. 3, 4, and 7.

Chester I. Barnard
1886–1961

*Mount Hermon Graduate about to
Start Study at Harvard University*

*Staff Expert on Rate Structures,
American Telephone and Telegraph
Company, 1910–1913*

The First President of New Jersey Bell
Telephone Company

Civic Leader, Author of
The Functions of the Executive,
and Thirty-year Veteran with the
American Telephone and
Telegraph Company
(twelve years as President of
the New Jersey Company)

President Herbert Hoover, Chester I. Barnard, and Former World Heavyweight Boxing Champion Gene Tunney Converse at the Boys Club Luncheon (Circa. 1940)

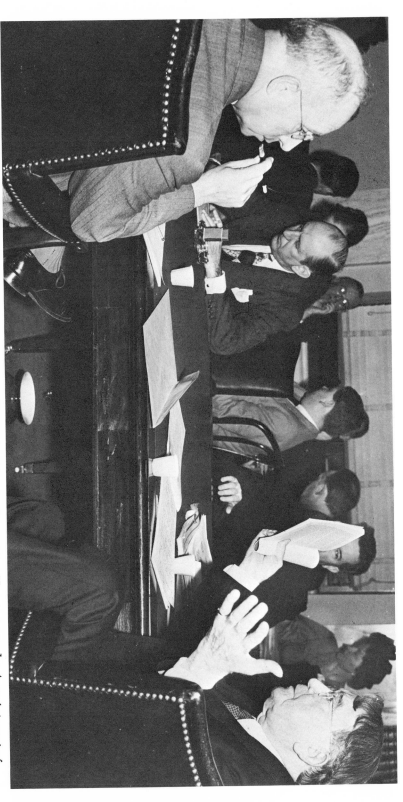

Senator Kenneth McKellar (D. Tenn.), Right, Questioning Barnard at Senate Committee Hearings on the Appointment of David E. Lilienthal as Chairman of the Atomic Energy Commission. Barnard Supported Lilienthal's Appointment

President of United Service Organization,
(U.S.O.) during World War II

John D. Rockefeller, Jr. (Left), Chester I. Barnard, and Walter Hoving,
President of Lord and Taylor (Circa. 1941)

*Mayor Robert Wagner of New York City Congratulates Chester I. Barnard
on His Appointment to the New York City Board of Health, October 1, 1957*

CONCEPT OF FORMAL ORGANIZATION

The above is a general introduction to the framework used by Chester I. Barnard. Of importance is his definition of formal organization and his recognition that formal organization while being a system exists as part of a more complex formal organization and that the executive organization arises to maintain communication and coordination of the various unit organizations which interact to give unity and wholeness to a complex organization.

In this presentation Barnard develops his concepts to show that organization is complex and that the executive functions develop from the very nature of complex organization. By focusing on environmental forces Barnard shows that the executive is not completely free to act. He faces limitations and prohibitions that restrict his range of activity. His environment places physical, biological, and social restraints upon his power of choice and his ability to act.

A Consideration of Individuals in Cooperative Systems

Barnard has defined organization as the consciously coordinated activities of two or more people. For organization to exist there must be two or more people who are willing to communicate and cooperate in attaining a stated purpose or goal. The building of a theory or organization requires consideration of what is known about people and their activities.

Individuals as Organizational Participants and as Whole Persons

The first thing to observe about people is that they differ. They differ in physical characteristics, innate capacities, and motivation. They also differ in personality: each person has his unique pattern for feeling, thinking, and acting. There is a tendency for us to view each individual as a single unique independent isolated whole thing. Only when we view people at a distance does this point of view tend to change. For example, when we talk of employees, students, workers, and so forth we think in abstract, general terms; but when we think of a personal friend or a member of our family the individual is seen as a unique personality. In thinking about people as contributors to an organization we have to differentiate between the individual as a total unique person and his role in the organization. Within an organization we depersonalize the individual. He is an employee or worker in a specific role with a defined activity to perform. It is specialization and division of labor of the activities of people that gives rise to organization. In the process the individual is called upon for a restricted, impersonal activity. The implicit idea of organization is that if each person performs his specialized duties and if the organization is properly designed,

67

the products of individual activity will come together in a coordinated manner and the organizational purpose will be achieved.

The need to depersonalize the individual arises from the fact that *his activities in organization are determined by the needs of the system. They are impersonal.* It should be recognized, however, that in any specific organizational setting the individual usually acts as a whole integrated human being. He brings his whole self to the organization and seldom limits his activities to the impersonal tasks established by his job description. As we will see later, a central problem of management is related to this difference between the individual as a whole person (that is, personal, subjective, and intuitive aspects of behavior) and his limited role within a specific organization (that is, rational, objective, and impersonal behavior).

Motives

People performing their organization roles must be motivated to act in the prescribed manner. After all, organization results from the modification of the actions of individuals and, thus, to understand organization it is helpful to be aware of the manner in which human beings modify or control behavior.

In a general sense we can think of individuals as being motivated by the desire to relieve tensions or satisfy needs. These needs may be biological (for example, shelter and food), social (for example, camaraderie), or psychological (for example, personal growth and self-esteem). With respect to needs, it is a biological fact that man possesses certain needs; the manner in which he satisfies them, however, is to a large measure culturally determined. "One man's feast may be another man's famine." Of strategic importance to the executive is the fact that the motivations of any specific individual are extremely complex. The individual himself is seldom fully aware of his own motivations. In fact, what a man desires is best inferred from what he does rather than what he says. Moreover, motives or drives are not stable. What is wanted under one set of conditions may not be sought under another set of circumstances. It is possible to influence motives by varying local conditions.

Free Will and Determinism

A problem encountered in the study of the behavior of people in organizations arises from consideration of the question of the degree to which individuals are free agents with the power to determine their own actions. The assumption is frequently made that the individual controls his own destiny, and thus we hold him responsible for his actions. We impute free will to the individual. Reflection upon man and his nature, however, indicates that what we are and what we do depends on all that is about us, upon inheritance, society, and forces in our environment. Man lacks complete free will. What he does, thinks, and feels depends not only on the exercise of his own will but also upon his ancestors, his biochemistry, and factors in his environment over which he has little or no control; and reality, thus, involves acceptance of some degree of determinism.

This fact poses a serious problem for the executive. If a man lacks free will can he be held responsible for his acts? Barnard's point of view is that the executive must recognize the absence of complete free will, but must, at the same time, assume free will to exist. Without the assumption of free will the concepts of personal integrity, legal responsibility, and moral responsibility cannot be meaningful.

Barnard sees the conflict of free will and determinism at the heart of many organizational problems. In essence it is the question of whether or not something controls a person or whether or not he can and should exert his own individuality. The position taken by Barnard is that both determinism and free will exist within an organization; however, he maintains that free will is essential for it is impossible to consider the individual in society or organization without moral responsibility. The justification of Barnard's position lies in the fact that the individual has the power of choice and is not completely controlled. The power of choice is the root of free will, individuality, and moral responsibility.

From the point of view of the executive the question of free will and determinism is important because it forces the recognition that, although it may be necessary to hold people accountable, there are many instances when a realistic appraisal of the situation would indicate that the individual in fact is not accountable. The executive should recognize that intelligent action in directing organization behavior involves changing the conditions of the environment, inculcating desired attitudes in people, and constructing appropriate incentives rather than erroneously blaming the individual for actions beyond his control.

Efficiency and Effectiveness

A key concept in Barnard's analysis of the individual concerns the sought and unsought results of organizational activities. The individual acting in the organization may achieve ends sought by the organization. Such activity is identified as *effective*. In contrast, the behavior directed toward organizational goals may also satisfy personal motives of the individual. To the extent that personal motives are satisfied the activity is considered *efficient*. Thus, activities occurring within organizations can and should be judged by two separate measures: *effectiveness* or the degree to which organization goals are attained at a minimum cost and *efficiency* or the individual's personal satisfaction derived from the activity.[14] The important deduction drawn from this dichotomy is that organization survival depends upon both effectiveness and efficiency. "Effectiveness relates to the accomplishment of the cooperative purpose, which is social and non-personal in character. Efficiency relates to the satisfaction of individual motives, and is personal in character."[15]

Without efficiency an organization cannot attract, hold, and motivate participants; without effectiveness it cannot justify its own existence. Thus, the executive's task involves maintaining effectiveness and efficiency. Even though these may not be determined by the same forces and may conflict.

Informal Organization

Up to this point we have been developing Barnard's theory of organization by focusing on formal organization and the general nature of individuals in cooperative systems. An important facet of formal organization is informal. Informal organization, however, needs to be differentiated from formal. Formal organization involves conscious coordination of activities of people and is impersonal in the sense that the activities of its members are determined by the needs of the organization, that is, the members play organizational roles. In contrast informal organization is personal and unconscious in the sense that it is not planned and is not dominated by the formally stated goals of the organization.

Informal organization is extremely difficult to define; it is more readily sensed or felt. It involves "learning the ropes" or knowing how to get along as a member of an organization, encompasses the unwritten laws of the organization, and involves knowing who's who, what's what, and why's why. It is evident in the folklore, mores, customs, traditions, and norms of conduct.

---

[14]This writer has simplified Barnard's discussion to be consistent with his basic dichotomy of the individual and the organization. In his writing, Barnard uses the terms *effective* and *efficiency* in two different contexts and as a result understanding of his presentation requires careful cross-reference to the framework or context in which he is referring to these terms. For example, at one time he identifies efficiency as related to acts not having negative unsought consequences relative to an individual's personal motives; at other times Barnard uses efficiency to refer to acts that satisfy the individual's personal motives. Compare *The Functions*, pp. 19, 20, 26, 43, 44, 55, 56, 82, and 235–239.

Barnard's choice of terms was unfortunate. In common usage efficiency connotes an input-output ratio and has meaning only as values are assigned to desired output. It would have been clearer for Barnard to have spoken of efficiency from the organizational viewpoint as contrasted with efficiency from the individual point of view.

[15]*The Functions*, p. 60.

Barnard defined informal organization as

> . . . the aggregate of personal contacts and interactions and associated groupings of people. . . .

> It may be regarded as a shapeless mass of quite varied densities, the variations in density being a result of external factors affecting the closeness of people geographically or of formal purposes which bring them specially into contact for conscious joint accomplishment.[16]

In other words, informal organization arises because of the interaction between people. It can arise from geographic, intellectual, task, or spiritual propinquity. The interaction between people tends to occur in repetitive and habitual ways. The result is that habitual ways of viewing things and common values as to right conduct or proper behavior develop. Informal organization grows and develops primarily without conscious planning. It is difficult for an outsider to discern, but it is felt by those who are actively part of the organization.

Barnard was one of the first organization theorists to examine closely the functional role of informal organization. Even today many executives respond to the observations that they have to deal with informal organization by asking "How can I get rid of it?" What they overlook is the fact that formal organization cannot exist without informal. Formal organizations are vitalized and conditioned by informal.[17]

Barnard found three important functions performed by informal organizations: (1) It facilitates communication. Informal organization is the aggregate of personal contacts between people. It involves experiences, attitudes, and emotions. Moreover, these contacts usually involve mutual likes and dislikes, mutual interests and inclinations. It is upon these that the all-important flow of communication is maintained throughout the organization. Moreover, *the informal organization is the mechanism by which issues which would otherwise require formal decisions and embarrassing action can be tactfully handled.* (2) It monitors and regulates the participation of individuals and in so doing maintains the stability of objective authority by influencing individual responsibility toward the acceptance of authority in the mutual interest. (3) The informal organization

---

[16]*Ibid.,* p. 115.

[17]At the time Barnard wrote, Mayo and Roethlisberger had drawn attention to some aspects of informal organization. Much of their work, however, focused upon the conflict between formal and informal. They did not emphasize the positive aspect and indispensability of the informal organization as Barnard did. See Elton Mayo, *The Human Problems of Industrial Civilization* (New York: Macmillan, 1933); T. N. Whitehead, *Leadership in a Free Society* (Cambridge: Harvard University Press, 1936); F. J. Roethlisberger and W. J. Dickson, *Management and the Worker,* Business Research Studies no. 9 (Cambridge: Harvard Graduate School of Business Administration, 1938).

provides a means for maintaining personal integrity and individualism within the formal organization. Informal organization is not dominated by impersonal goals or by formal authority. Rather it is "characterized by choice and [furnishes] the opportunity. . . . for reinforcement of attitudes."[18] It is an avenue by which the whole person can function as an integrated individual rather than only in a limited organizational role.[19]

Informal organization is the safety valve which prevents the complete depersonalization of the contributor to a cooperative system.

In the final analysis, Barnard says, formal organization cannot exist for long without informal. Formal organization provides the skeletal structure. It is impersonal. In contrast informal organization provides the energy and driving force and is personal.

---

[18]*The Functions,* p. 122.

[19]This point has been developed by Philip Selznick, "Foundations of the Theory of Organization," *American Sociological Review* 13 (February 1948): 25–35. This article has been reprinted in Wolf, *Management: Readings Toward a General Theory,* pp. 38–52.

V.

Aspects of Formal Organization

Formal organizations can be studied from many points of view. We can study them as decision-making and decision-implementing cooperative systems, as incentive systems, as moral systems, and so forth. Each such point of view is incomplete, yet each adds to our understanding of what organizations and their common features are. In this chapter we summarize Barnard's central concepts regarding perspectives for viewing formal organization. Barnard labeled these "elements." His elements may be classified as specialization, incentives, authority, decision, status systems, and morals.[1]

Specialization

Barnard draws attention to the fact that organization and specialization are in many ways synonymous. In his discussion he emphasizes "(I) that the effectiveness of cooperative systems depends almost entirely upon the invention or adoption of *innovations* of specialization; and (II) that the primary aspect of specialization is the *analysis of purpose* or general ends into intermediate or detailed ends which are means to the more remote ends."[2]

Barnard observes that the specialization in organizations may be along five lines: "(a) the place where work is done [geographic specialization]; (b) the time at which work which is done [temporal]; (c) the persons with whom work is done [associational]; (d) the things upon which work is done [functional]; (e) the method or process by which work is done [processual]."[3]

He points out that scheduling and sequencing activities are fundamental to effective organization and, in addition, that acts must of necessity be spatially specialized. Two people cannot occupy the identical place at

---

[1]This classification is based on Barnard's work, but is essentially that of the author. Further subdivision is possible; for example, Barnard never discussed communication as an isolated phenomenon, instead he wove it into almost all phases of his other comments.

[2]*The Functions*, p. 132. Emphasis in original.

[3]*Ibid.*, p. 128–129.

the same time. Action must be in the right place at the right time if organization is to be effective. Barnard also highlights the importance of specialization with respect to persons with whom work is done. This associational specialization is a fundamental aspect of informal organization and involves knowing the people one works with and feeling rapport with them. Barnard considers this one of the most important aspects of the executive organization.

Barnard's discussion of specialization helps to illustrate his theory of formal organization. To him formal organizations consist of the consciously coordinated activities of two or more persons directed toward achieving some goals or a goal. The formal organization exists because of the limitations of individuals in dealing with their environment (for example, one man is not strong enough to achieve a goal or he cannot be in two or more places at once, and so forth). Two of the essential aspects of formal organization are determining the correct sequence of activities (coordination by time or temporal specialization) and determining where each act shall occur (effective location of acts or geographic specialization). Having the right action at the right time in the right place is essential to effective organization, but is dependent upon bringing together persons who are willing to submit to the requirements of coordination and are able to communicate adequately. Adequate communication involves social specialization or associational specialization. To Barnard, thus, associational specialization, along with geographic and temporal, is of strategic importance to organization. Barnard, however, is consistent with his previously developed theory of formal organization; he recognizes that specialization may involve a variety of lines and numerous combinations and, although he emphasizes time, place, and association, sees these existing in a system of mutual dependency with other aspects of specialization. They are part of a system of coordinated activities.

Probably one of Barnard's most significant points with respect to his discussion of specialization is his emphasis on the fact that complex organization is composed of specialized subunits which are, to a large degree, autonomous. For example, Barnard states that, "Each unit organization has a specific objective, specific locational characteristics, specific time schedule, and involves a specific associational situation which determines the selection of individual contributors."[4]

He again emphasized this point twenty-three years after publishing *The Functions.* Its implications were noted by Barnard when he was asked: "What would be your approach in teaching men who are training for management?" He replied:

---

[4]*Ibid.,* p. 136.

I would say that the most fruitful approach is to start with the understanding that if any collection of individuals is formed into a group (whether it's spontaneous, a spontaneously organized group, or one that is nominally designed), once in operation it is very largely autonomous. The function of the formal aspects is like that of a skeleton in the body. What you are mostly concerned with is the physiology of the relationships involved but first of all you have to know anatomy well enough to know that there is a skeleton and that it keeps in place the organs which are mostly going to function autonomously. Now, the idea of autonomous groups is anathema to businessmen, theoretical military men, and I'm sure to the intellectuals as a group. They continue to talk about the formalities of the organization as if that were fundamentally the subject with which you're dealing. My approach would be to recognize that that's not the case. The case is that you're dealing with groups that largely are, and almost inevitably have to be, autonomous. You cannot direct from the top the multifarious activities of the groups down below. There has to be a reaction and a response to local conditions that can't be conveyed by anybody at a distance.[5]

Recognition of the autonomous nature of unit organization led Barnard to observe that "purpose is the unifying element of formal organization."[6] Barnard reasoned that the problem of managing involves the coordination of specialized parts or units so that the purposes or goals of the formal organization may be accomplished by redefining and breaking those purposes into parts. These detailed purposes are assigned to subunits of the organization. The coordination of the unit organizations, thus, involves achievement of specialized purposes in a proper time sequence so that all of the activities of the complex organization are coordinated.

For Barnard's framework an important aspect of management is understanding the relation of the general purpose of complex organizations to specialized purposes of unit organizations. It is not essential that general purpose be understood or accepted, but only that specialized purpose at the unit level be known and accepted. If the detailed purpose of the unit organization is not known or is not accepted the unit organization will disintegrate. Of course, if the specialized purpose of the unit organization can be presented in relation to the general purpose and if detailed purpose can be shown to be fundamental to the achievement of the overall goal of the formal organization, it is likely that the motivations of participants at the unit level will be intensified. It should be recognized, however, that "It is

---

[5]William B. Wolf, "Precepts for Managers: Interviews with Chester I. Barnard," *California Management Review* 6 (Fall 1963): 93.

[6]*The Functions*, p. 137.

belief in cause rather than intellectual understanding of the objective which is of chief importance."[7]

Barnard's analysis of specialization points to the importance of time, space, and association. Probably more significantly, it focuses on the autonomous nature of the unit organizations which interact and are coordinated to constitute complex organization. The relative independence of unit organizations leads to analysis of purpose and the need to redefine general purpose so specialized purpose for each unit of organization is arrived at and accepted.

Incentives

An essential aspect of organization is the willingness of persons to contribute their individual efforts to the cooperative system. Thus an important point of view for studying organizations is that of incentives. The individual is always the basic strategic factor in organization and he must be induced to cooperate, or there cannot be a formal organization.[8] This has been noted in our discussion of efficiency.[9]

Barnard sees a variety of incentives in organizations. Each involves costs and revenues; thus, the organization problem involves applying the varying incentive systems in a manner in which marginal revenue is equal to marginal costs. The problem is complicated by the variety of systems, the instability in the various incentives, and the mutual dependency of the various incentives upon each other. Moreover, the effectiveness of incentives is a function of the broader environment, the effectiveness of organization effort, the internal efficiency of organization, and the amount of inducements paid. If the organization pays out more than it receives it cannot then continue to offer inducements.

In his analyses Barnard develops a system of classification for incentives which differentiates between attempts to satisfy the needs of individuals and to change the needs of individuals. Underlying his discussion is a simple equation in which he sees individuals as motivated to contribute to organizations by the net satisfactions arising from their activities. Such net satisfaction exists when the positive advantages from a specific activity are greater than the disadvantages.[10]

---

[7]*Ibid.*, p. 138.

[8]*Ibid.*, pp. 139–160. For the development of a general theory of organization stimulated by Barnard's concepts see Peter B. Clark and James Q. Wilson, "Incentive Systems: A Theory of Organizations," *Administrative Science Quarterly* 6 (September 1961): 129–166.

[9]See p. 70 of this work.

[10]It should be recognized that individuals generally "feel" rather than logically weigh advantages and disadvantages.

Barnard concludes that individuals may be motivated by increasing the positive advantages associated with an activity or by decreasing the disadvantages. He points out, however, that despite the usefulness of such an equation for conceptualizing motivation the fact is that in reality it is difficult to tell which aspect is affected by a specific act. For example, improving working conditions may both increase the positive advantages of work and reduce the disadvantages.

Barnard classifies the systems of incentives as those which appeal to the existing state of persons' minds and those which change the state of mind. In other words, he sees people as having needs which can be satisfied or else as being malleable so that their needs may be changed. The first of these types of incentives he calls objective incentives which are devices for satisfying existing needs. The use of such incentives he calls the method of incentives. In contrast, Barnard identifies the use of more subjective incentives, those designed to change attitudes, as the *method of persuasion*. In commercial enterprises one generally finds that the method of incentives is emphasized. The method of persuasion, however, is also important and although it is not formally emphasized it is used. In the long run both methods tend to be ineffective because of the natural dispersive tendency of individuals and the competition between various organizations for the contributions of individuals.

Method of Incentive[11]

To Barnard "the egotistical motives of self-preservation and of self-satisfaction are dominating forces."[12] Much of the effort to motivate individuals appeals to these. He notes that many incentives involve specific inducements to cooperate; these include material inducements, personal nonmaterial opportunities, desirable physical conditions, and ideal benefaction. In addition Barnard distinguishes what he calls general incentives which are not personal and cannot be specifically offered.[13] The general incentives are associational attractiveness, adaptation of conditions to habitual methods and attitudes, the opportunity for enlarged participation, and the condition of communion.

Material inducements are tangible and include physical conditions, things, or money offered as rewards for contributions from individuals. Barnard maintained that our society cultivates a love of material things and because of this most individuals feel that they should seek material

---

[11]Compare *The Functions*, pp. 142–149.

[12]*Ibid.*, p. 139.

[13]Here again Barnard uses the differentiation between individual (personal) and collective (impersonal) to organize his thinking. This key differentiation underlies many of his concepts.

benefits. The desire for material things has been inculcated into us and, thus, we have helped perpetuate an illusion that beyond the subsistence level material incentives are most effective. In reality, above the minimum necessities of life, the unaided power of material incentives is exceedingly limited. In fact,

> . . . many of the most effective and powerful organizations are built upon incentives in which the materialistic elements, above bare subsistence, are either relatively lacking or absolutely absent. Military organizations have been relatively lacking in material incentives. The greater part of the work of political organizations is without material incentive.[14]

Barnard points out, however, that in a pecuniary society such as ours money is more than a material inducement. Money may be used as an indirect means of satisfying nonmaterialistic motives and is in itself a symbol of status and success.

Personal nonmaterial opportunities consist of things such as prestige, distinction, personal position. In many instances they are more important as incentives than material inducements. Barnard's experience indicates that money without position, distinction or prestige is utterly ineffective. For short periods of time men will even serve for distinction with inferior material rewards. Moreover, it is apparent that the real value of money reward is frequently the differential amount which indicates distinction of rank. Differences in money income within an organization become a source of jealousy and disruption if not accompanied by other factors of prestige and distinction.

"Desirable physical conditions of work are often important conscious, and more often important unconscious, inducements to cooperation."[15]

Ideal benefactions involve the satisfaction of personal ideals and include such things as pride of workmanship, patriotism, aesthetic sense, and religious feelings. They are among the most powerful incentives of cooperation, yet are among the most neglected in the business world. Barnard believes that ideal benefactions are among the most forceful incentives. Underlying this incentive is the concept that a person's self-esteem is paramount in his commitment. Those benefactions which raise self-esteem or reinforce it are positive motivations. This theme is developed in Barnard's discussion of loyalty. He points out that the service rendered is frequently the crucial aspect of loyalty. Individuals should be asked to be loyal to what they do, that is to the service, and not be asked to assume blind loyalty to the organization. He observes:

---

[14]*The Functions*, p. 144.
[15]*Ibid.*, p. 146.

But in the hundreds and hundreds of talks I've made . . . I never talked about loyalty to the company, *never!* I don't think that you can be loyal to a corporation. If you can, I don't think you can sell it to the ordinary person. *I always talked about the loyalty of the organization or loyalty to the service* and believe me, it's very effective.[16]

Among the general incentives associational attractiveness involves personal and social compatibility. It is one of the most important general inducements offered to individuals. Its relative importance is more generally felt than openly and logically stated. The fact is that an essential bond of organizations is communication and unless men feel a compatibility both the formal and informal channels of communication tend to fail. Adaptation of conditions to habitual methods and attitudes is an important general incentive which is recognized in the attitude that those trained in foreign methods are not likely to do well. It recognizes that frequently such people are not likely to attempt to cooperate.

The opportunity for enlarged participation in the course of events is often of controlling importance. "Its realization is the feeling of importance of the result of effort because of the importance of the cooperative effort as a whole."[17] The condition of communion is a general incentive related to social compatibility. "It is the feeling of personal comfort in social relations that is sometimes called solidarity. . . . "[18] It involves comradeship brotherhood, and mutual support for personal attitudes.

In Barnard's view the method of incentive, satisfying the existing needs of individuals, can never adequately move men to cooperate. He bases this conclusion upon the observations that different men are moved by different incentives, men are unstable in their desires, and there are economic limits on the use of material incentives. Thus, Barnard concludes that organizations must resort to changing the desires of men so that the incentives offered will be adequate.

Method of Persuasion

Persuasion is a fundamental incentive in complex organization. Barnard discusses it under three groupings: the creation of coercive conditions, the rationalization of opportunity, and the inculcation of motives.

Coercion involves varying degrees of exclusion from the organization. It creates fear among those not directly excluded so that they will make the required contributions to the organization. The degree of exclusion

---

[16]Wolf, "Precepts for Managers," p. 92. For further development of this theme see Barnard, "Twenty-five Years" (Address to the Fifteenth Annual Assembly of the Telephone Pioneers of America, New York, New York, October 23, 1936).

[17]*The Functions*, pp. 147–148.

[18]*Ibid.*, p. 148.

varies from discharge to ostracism to withholding specific benefits. It is an expression of the power of organizations to persuade by force and it gives notice to all who participate that certain acts or violations of policy are intolerable and bring punishment.

The rationalization of opportunity involves attempting to convince individuals that they ought to contribute to formal organization. Barnard points out that "people will not work for what they are not convinced is 'worth while.' "[19] Hence, rationalization is an important aspect of incentives. Two kinds of rationalization of opportunity are encountered, generalized and specific. The generalized aspects of rationalization of opportunity involve salesmanship, advertising, and propaganda. Specific rationalization involves personal appeal to contribute to an organization on the basis that the experience will be more satisfying than other available choices.

The inculcation of motives is the form of persuasion that is most important. It involves deliberate education of the young and propaganda for adults. It also involves learning by precept and example. It is, thus, one of the most difficult aspects of persuasion with which to deal; yet, it is at the heart of the culture of nations and societies. More often than not the learned patterns of behavior (motives and values) are the greatest limitations to which organizations must adapt their processes in administering incentives.

The contribution of Barnard's rudimentary theory of incentives lies in the manner in which he has developed the subject as well as in some of his new emphases. Most important is the fact that when incentives are viewed within Barnard's framework it is at once apparent that the problem of adequate incentives in organization is complex. Barnard has summed up this conclusion as follows:

> . . . excepting in rare instances, the difficulties of securing the means of offering incentives, of avoiding conflict of incentives, and of making effective persuasive efforts, are inherently great; and that the determination of the precise combination of incentives and of persuasion that will be both effective and feasible is a matter of great delicacy. Indeed, it is so delicate and complex that rarely, if ever, is the scheme of incentives determinable in advance of application. It can only evolve; and the questions relating to it become chiefly those of strategic factors from time to time in the course of the life of the organization. It is also true, of course, that the scheme of incentives is probably the most unstable of the elements of the cooperative system, since invariably external conditions affect the possibilities of material incentives; and human motives are likewise highly variable. Thus incentives represent

---

[19]*Ibid.*, p. 151.

the final residual of all the conflicting forces involved in organization, a very slight change in underlying forces often making a great change in the power of incentives; and yet it is only by the incentives that the effective balancing of these forces is to be secured, if it can be secured at all.[20]

It is from the difficulty of the problem of incentives that Barnard sees two organization practices developing. First is the propensity of all organizations to grow. Growth offers opportunity for the realization of all kinds of incentives and, thus, is sought as a way of dealing with the insoluble problem of incentives. Second is the inherent difficulty of securing adequate incentives which leads to highly selective recruiting of personnel. The process involves the maintenance of different incentives so that the distribution of incentives is in proportion to the value and effectiveness of the various contributions sought.

In summary, incentives pose one of the fundamental problems of complex organizations. In final analysis, the problem is part of the basic dichotomy of the individual and the collectivity. Individual incentives must be personal and subjective and must motivate individuals to contribute their efforts to the cooperative system. This is a highly personal decision and incentives need to account for this personal equation. Incentives, however, are applied in a system of mutual causality in which everything depends upon everything else. In such a system incentives have to be seen in terms of their multiple effects. To reward one individual may be at the same time to punish others. For example, if an individual is working with a group in a simple organization and the boss decides that he should be rewarded by an increase in pay, then the difference between his wages and those of his fellow workers is changed. The other workers are apt to respond by saying "Why did he get an increase while we didn't?" The reward to one individual may motivate him but, at the same time, reduce the morale and productivity of his fellow workers.

Furthermore, incentives have costs associated with them. It is almost impossible to measure precisely the return and the cost of the various systems of incentives. By logical analysis, however, we know that such reasoning does apply and that if people are not motivated to produce or if the cost of motivating people consumes all of the resources of the organization then the organization cannot exist.

The history of man in society, as the history of men in organizations, shows that differentiation among contributors is a fundamental aspect of incentives. There is thus little likelihood that differentiation will be eliminated and the question of incentives is thus bounded by the dichotomy of

---

[20]*Ibid.*, pp. 158–159.

the individual and the organization or individualism and collectivism. It is a problem which appears insoluble; yet, it is a problem which we attack by seeking approximate solutions and maintaining flexibility in our attempts to deal with it.

The difficulty of dealing with incentives leads to a number of pressures within the organization. First is the pressure toward continued expansion. Expansion is a way of mitigating numerous problems of incentives. It allows a general movement up the ladder and a feeling of accomplishment. Second is the recruiting of individuals at different levels in order to maintain differentials.

Authority

Barnard presents a third perspective for viewing formal organization, that of the authority system. Barnard's comments on authority have caused considerable debate. Unfortunately this debate has been couched in terms that tended to distort the real development of a theory of organization and management. In essence, the polemic has focused upon the source of the managerial right to command subordinates. Barnard is frequently identified as representing the acceptance theory of authority which holds that managerial authority rests upon the consent of subordinates. In contrast, many writers emphasize that management has the right to command and see managers as being given formal power within the organization. This authority is seen as coming from superior organizations or higher levels within formal organization. In other words, authority is seen as delegated downward from higher levels.[21] In this view formal authority is the power transmitted from basic social institutions downward through a hierarchy to the individual manager.

Unfortunately in the debate over the nature of authority Barnard was the stimulus rather than an active participant. He never directly rebutted those who attacked his position. Before his death he pointed out that his book put "too much emphasis on authority" and not enough on responsibility.

Authority Defined

Barnard defines authority as "the character of a communication (order) in a formal organization by virtue of which it is accepted by a contributor to the organization as governing the action he contributes; that is, as gov-

---

[21]The intensity of the debate is an interesting phenomenon. The distortion is understandable since Barnard has been misquoted and misrepresented as saying that managers really do not manage.

erning or determining what he does or is not to do so far as the organization is concerned."[22]

With respect to this definition it should be emphasized that Barnard is
talking about the characteristic of an order and not the power of a person
or the rights of a position. Moreover, according to this definition authority
involves two aspects: the accepting of a communication or order as authoritative which is subjective, personal, and an individual matter and
the character of the communication by virtue of which it is accepted which
is objective and strongly controlled by organizational factors. Finally,
Barnard's definition leads to the conclusion that "the decision as to whether
an order has authority or not lies with the persons to whom it is addressed,
and does not reside in 'persons of authority' or those who issue these
orders."[23]

The Authoritative Order

The acceptance of an order or communication as authoritative is a subjective matter. It depends not only on the formalities of the communication, but also on the individual who receives it. With respect to the individual or subjective aspect of authority, Barnard points out that an individual in an organization can assent to orders only if they are understood,
if the individual interprets them as consistent with the purpose of the
organization, and if, at the same time, he is able to comply and does not
interpret his actions as detrimental to his personal interests.

Cooperation within formal organization endures because of three circumstances which usually surround communications: Orders are usually
understood, and compliance is visualized, as being in both organizational
and individual interest; in addition, the individual is usually able to comply. Each individual has what Barnard has identified as a "zone of indifference," within which orders are acceptable and not consciously challenged. Group pressure within formal organization tends to maintain the
individual's zone of indifference.

The concept of a zone of indifference needs to be elaborated upon. It
refers to orders that are unquestionably accepted and is usually related to
what the contributor assumed to be the obligations he assumed in joining
the cooperative effort. On taking his job the individual has certain expectations and he implicitly delegates to his superiors the right to issue cer-

---

[22]*The Functions*, p. 163.
[23]*Ibid*. It should be pointed out that Barnard's thinking about authority was stimulated
by Eugene Ehrlich's *Fundamental Principles of the Sociology of Law*, trans. by W. L.
Moll (New York: Russell & Russell, 1936). The theme of this work is that the sources of
law lie in the people and not in the legislatures, courts, or formally designated rulers.
Compare *The Functions*, p. x.

tain orders. When orders are issued which are consistent with this expectation the subordinate accepts them. An individual's zone of indifference will be a function of his commitment to the organization, as well as of the burdens associated with the carrying out of each specific order.

Closely related to the above is the pressure which develops within the organization to maintain the objective authority of communications. Denying authority to orders threatens the survival of formal organization. Most of the contributors in an organization, thus, have an active personal interest in maintaining the authority of all orders which they interpret as being within their zone of indifference. This is an important function of informal organization. Informal organization affects the attitudes of individuals and establishes the generally accepted norm for the acceptability of orders.

The Fiction of Superior Authority

Barnard maintained that the concept of superior authority is a fiction which is useful to formal organization:

> ... the common sense of the community informally arrived at affects the attitude of individuals, and makes them, as individuals, loath to question authority that is within or near the zone of indifference. ...

> This fiction [that authority comes down from above] merely establishes a presumption among individuals in favor of the acceptability of orders from superiors, enabling them to avoid making issues of such orders without incurring a sense of personal subserviency or a loss of personal or individual status with their fellows. ...

> The fiction of superior authority ... makes it possible ... to treat a personal question impersonally.[24]

Barnard points out that the concept of superior authority is a way for the individual to avoid the assumption of personal responsibility. It allows a type of delegation of responsibility to those who are allegedly in authority and thereby allows those who delegate the authority and responsibility upward to escape what they tend to be reluctant to assume, responsibility for their own actions in the organization. Finally, the belief in superior authority provides a means for preserving the good of the organization. It gives notice that the good of the organization is at stake and is affected by the degree to which individuals assent to orders. To deny the authority of an organizational communication is to threaten all individuals who derive net advantage as members of the organization.

---

[24]*The Functions*, pp. 169–170.

84

Precepts Regarding Authority

On the basis of his analysis of the acceptance of orders Barnard framed observations which can be identified as precepts. They are rough guides which should help executives in securing acceptance of orders.

1. Interpret orders for individuals and groups. A considerable part of the executive job is the interpretation and reinterpretation of orders so that they are applicable and are understood in concrete circumstances. It is impossible to take into account all local conditions; hence, flexibility in presenting and interpreting orders is essential if their general purposes are to be achieved. If the order is out of context and not intelligible to recipients it cannot have authority.

2. Avoid conflicting orders. Such a situation requires denying authority to one of the orders and this can undermine objective authority.

3. Never issue orders which cannot or will not be obeyed.

4. When it appears necessary to issue orders which are apparently unacceptable, the executive should prepare the way by preliminary persuasion and education and by offering inducements so that there is less chance of participants denying the authority of the orders.

5. Recognize that attention should be focused upon responsibility rather than authority. This is a point made by Barnard shortly before his death:

> In my opinion, the great weakness of my book is that it doesn't deal adequately with the question of responsibility and its delegation. The emphasis is too much on authority, which is the subordinate subject. Now, all the teaching in business circles, and most of them in military and academic circles, is wrong from my standpoint. The emphasis is put on authority which, to me now, is a secondary derivative set up.[25]

The executive should recognize the relation of authority to responsibility. Barnard summarized this as follows:

> I can say, "I now hold you responsible for this," but if you don't accept that then there's nothing I can do about it. . . . You can dissemble, you can give me the runaround, but if you don't accept it, it just doesn't work. Now if you stop to think of it, almost everything that's done does not depend much on the formal requirements, as it does in real estate transactions, for instance, and does not in stock exchange transactions. . . . If you take into account that factor, you find nearly everything depends upon the moral commitment. I'm perfectly confident

---

[25]*Conversations,* p. 15. In these interviews Barnard also observed that there had been almost no discussion of responsibility by social scientists and added, "If I were active and had the mood to do it, what I would do next would be to deal with the subject of responsibility: what we mean by it and who's involved in it, the importance of delegation, why the delegation has to precede any question of authority" (p. 23).

that, with occasional lapses, that if I make a date with you, whom I have never met, you'll keep it and you'll feel confident that I'll keep it; and there's absolutely nothing binding that makes us do it. And yet the world runs on that — you just couldn't run a college, you couldn't run a business, you couldn't run a church, couldn't do anything except on the basis of the moral commitments that are involved in what we call responsibility. You can't operate a large organization unless you can delegate responsibility, not authority but responsibility. Authority comes second. One factor in authority, formal authority, to which I have seen no attention given by anybody is that it is protective of the people who have accepted moral responsibility. Let me illustrate that in the case of a vast amount of salesmanship in this country: you say to John Jones, "This is your district," and by any authoritative creation of the position, you say to everybody else "Keep out. You don't belong." See? Therefore, the authoritative aspect of the assignment is the protection of the man in it, and this goes to quite strange extremes sometimes. I bought a dictaphone apparatus here — I have a part-time secretary. She lives in Brooklyn and I live here in Manhattan. A dictaphone set-up involves the recording end of it and then the pick-up end of it which the stenographer uses. It's a separate instrument. Because the pick-up end, if that's the right term for it, was to remain in Brooklyn, I had to write two checks. I had to make two deals; one was for the input end in Manhattan, and the other was for the output end in Brooklyn, because that was the prerogative of the Brooklyn organization.[26]

6. Recognize the limits of the saying that "authority and responsibility should be equal." Barnard held that frequently one has responsibility without authority. He develops this point in a 1944 review of *The Elements of Administration* by Col. Lyndall Urwick:

Mr. Urwick gives renewed currency to the ancient bromide: "Authority and responsibility are correlative." He says, "It is of great importance to smooth working that at all levels authority and responsibility should be coterminous and equal." No statement in the whole gamut of twiddle-twaddle about administration seems to me so misleading as this; yet its equivalent can be heard as gospel in almost any organization. Such nonsense appears to derive from failure to observe common behavior or to discriminate between authority to command and authority to act, including to persuade, to convince, to influence, to sell. Certainly no one may justly be held responsible for the specific behavior of a particular third party without authority to command that party; but, in general, most men are held responsible for results as to which no authority to command that party; but, in general, most men are held responsible for results as to which no authority can be given. Salesmen are given authority to sell and are held responsible for sales, but obviously cannot be given authority to compel purchases. In any kind of organization good executives know how to get action for which they cannot be given authority to command. Nothing is more important to teach the beginner than this. It does not gainsay the necessity for a scalar system of command. It merely affirms as a matter of plain observation and common experience that in any organization, not a moribund bureaucracy, the measure of responsibility exceeds the measure of authority to command; and that in most organizations many members of high and low degree are properly held accountable and responsible who have little or no authority of command.[27]

Insuring the Acceptance of an Order

We have been discussing the subjective aspects of authority. It is an aspect with which the executive is generally not predominately occupied. Rather the executive is more concerned with the objective character of a communication inducing acceptance — with what action he can take to secure authority for his communications. With respect to this we should start by pointing to the setting in which authority is being discussed. We are concerned with acts of executives, which are official acts and have meaning only within formal organization. Individuals are able to exercise formal authority only when they are acting officially. An important part of establishing the authority of a communication, thus, involves establishing its official character by particular attention to such things as time, place, dress, ceremony, and authentication. Since authoritative communications are official and apply only to members of the organization, the executive has no formal authority outside of his jurisdiction.

Of course, authority depends upon a cooperative personal attitude of individuals as discussed above but it also depends on the organizational system of communication in the organization. The system of communication is vital to effectiveness and efficiency, that is, to organizational survival. Under the name "lines of authority," this system of communication is a continuing problem of formal organization. With respect to the formal organization's system of communication Barnard observes:

1. "A communication has the presumption of authority when it originates at sources of organization information."[28] Such a source tends to carry more weight if it is a communication center rather than an individual (it is impersonal rather than personal), if the communication is within the recognized scope or jurisdiction of the center, and if the communication is in tune with the actual situation confronting the recipient of it.

---

[27]Chester I. Barnard, "Review of *The Elements of Administration* by L. Urwick," *Personnel* 21 (January 1945): 257–258.
[28]*The Functions*, p. 173.

2. A communication can also have the authority of leadership which is imputed to men of knowledge and understanding. Authority of leadership reinforces that of position and tends to build confidence among recipients that increases acceptance. It is important, however, to recognize the difference between superior position and superior personal ability. When a person of superior ability lacks formal position his advice (communications) is taken at the risk of the taker. Such a person has influence rather than authority. There cannot be authority without corresponding responsibility.

3. To maintain objective authority the channels of communication should definitely be known. "The lines of authority must be definitely established"[29] through job definitions, official notices of assignments of positions, organization charts, and general educational devices such as staff meetings, house organs, and so forth.

4. To maintain an objective authority it is essential that everyone have a definite formal relation to the organization. Everyone must report to someone.

5. Problems of communication require that "the line of communication be as direct or short as possible."[30] Language is ambiguous and thus susceptible to misunderstanding. Moreover, transmitting messages from one unit to another results in losses and additions. The tendency is for content to become progressively more general as it goes up the organizational hierarchy and to become more specific as it descends. As the lines of communication become extended there is a tendency for them to slow down and for errors in transmission to increase. Executives may maintain short lines of communication by innovation in organizational design, for example, the use of staff assistants, the use of functional staffs, and decentralization of responsibility.

6. In order to avoid conflicting communications the general practice should be to use the complete line of communication. If the line is jumped there are apt to be errors of interpretation and difficulty in maintaining responsibility. In a talk to the Committee on Work in Industry of the National Research Council, Barnard illustrated this precept from his experience as director of emergency relief in the state of New Jersey.

One of the rules pretty generally followed in organizations of large size is not to "jump" the line of organization in passing out orders or getting information. If you have an order from the top you give it through the line, and information from the bottom comes through the line. You avoid this sometimes skillfully and artistically, but as a rule it is neces-

[29]*Ibid.*, pp. 175–176.
[30]*Ibid.*, p. 176.

sary to follow the line. I thought in the particular instance of the relief organization that I was dealing with people who had not been inoculated with high organization practice. I suspected that the reactions we had to take into account in established organizations were artificial, and when I found it convenient to do so with the relief organization I went directly to the local man, and thus attempted to save trouble for everybody. Nevertheless, I found that what happened was exactly what would have happened in the telephone organization if I had done it there — personalities, emotion, diffusion of responsibility, etc.[31]

7. The executives serving as communication centers must have adequate competency. By this Barnard means that they must be capable of discriminating and discerning incoming messages so that they can be translated into outgoing communications which meet the needs of their organizations. Adequacy in this area requires a certain amount of general ability to sense the organization as a whole as well as technical knowledge and knowledge of the capabilities of personalities and a sense of the informal organization. In large complex organizations the problem of maintaining competency at communication centers is almost beyond the capacity of any one individual. Thus, in such organizations one finds that major communication centers have to be elaborately organized with staffs, deputies, assistants, and so forth. Moreover, one finds that for the most important complex organizations highest objective authority is lodged in a board, committee, or other organized executive group rather than an individual executive.

8. While an organization is functioning, the line of communication should not be interrupted. To insure that the line of communication is uninterrupted it is a practice to consider the office more important than the man and to make special arrangements to see that positions are automatically filled when the individuals who usually occupy them are unable to do so. Such action is necessary because specific communications cannot otherwise be attended to and also, "the *informal* organization disintegrates very quickly if the formal 'line of authority' is broken. In organization parlance, 'politics' runs riot."[32]

9. Every communication should be authenticated. It is essential that when a person issues an order his position in the organization is known and the order is within his competence. The ways of doing this vary from organization to organization. One way is by ceremonials of investiture, inaugurations, swearings-in, inductions, and so forth. Such procedures aid in the creation of acceptance by subordinates. Moreover, "dignifying the

---

[31]Committee on Work in Industry of the National Research Council, *Fatigue of Workers: Its Relation to Industrial Production* (New York: Reinhold, 1941), p. 137.

[32]*The Functions,* p. 180. Emphasis in original.

superior position is an important method of dignifying *all* connection with organization. . . . "[33]

Barnard's discussion of authority is closely related to other aspects of coordination in formal organizations. As he uses the term "Authority is another name for the willingness and capacity of individuals to submit to the necessities of cooperative systems."[34] It cannot be separated from the other aspects of organization. Communication, specialization, incentive, and purpose are all aspects comprehended in coordination. With understanding of Barnard's analysis of authority, the debates of a theory of superior authority *versus* an acceptance theory of authority become minor and instead the question of delegation and acceptance of responsibility becomes the important consideration.

Decisions

If one were to attempt to select the area of Chester I. Barnard's major impact on the study of organization and management he would undoubtedly point to decision theory. Barnard himself observed:

> I think Herbert Simon and most of the others got the idea of the importance of decision making from my book. Nobody at that time was talking about decision making. The psychologists weren't, the social-psychologists weren't, and the business management people weren't, and I put a good deal of emphasis upon it.[35]

The role of decision processes in Barnard's theory of organization centers on the concept of choice. Decision making involves acts of choice

---

[33]*Ibid.*, p. 181. Emphasis in original.

[34]*Ibid.*, p. 184.

[35]*Conversations*, p. 46. A careful reading of Simon's *Administrative Behavior: A Study of Decision-Making Processes in Administrative Organization* (New York: Macmillan, 1957) reveals the strong influence Barnard had. Simon states, "To Mr. Chester I. Barnard I owe a special debt: first for his own book, *The Functions of the Executive*, which has been a major influence upon my thinking about administration; secondly, for the extremely careful critical review which he gave to the preliminary version of his book; and finally, for his Foreword to the present edition" (pp. xlvii–xlviii).

There is reason, however, to suspect that Barnard's observation is not completely accurate. For example, Simon points out that in the early thirties there was a great deal of activity in statistics, microeconomics, and psychology which involved decision theory. Among others, he cites the work of R. A. Fisher, Karl Pearson, Frank Knight, Kurt Lewin, and Otto Selz. Moreover, Simon points out that he had a long-standing interest in decision theory. He studied it in courses at the University of Chicago and in 1936 he used a decision-making approach to management in evaluations of municipal fire department operations. Simon concludes that, although he can understand Barnard's observation, a more critical review of the situation reveals that the introduction of decision making as the central administrative process is part of a much larger intellectual revolution associated with the growth of symbolic logic (Letter from Herbert Simon to William B. Wolf, March 3, 1969).

between alternatives. In a general sense Barnard's conception of organization can be redefined in terms of the choices made by those whose interactions and activities constitute the organization. For example, we can describe organization in terms of decisions about specialization and division of labor. Such decisions are intimately related to decisions regarding general goals and purposes. If we assume that general purposes are given and the formal structure is also established, we can then describe formal organization in terms of the acceptance of authority by which contributors perform organizational tasks and have their activities coordinated. Coordination is performed primarily by executives who make decisions as to courses of action and issue orders which lead to the integration of the activities of the specialized parts so that the organization functions as a system.

Logical and Nonlogical Thought Processes

A starting place for the discussion of Barnard's contribution to decision theory is his interest in subconscious, intuitive reasoning. The theme of much of Barnard's writing is that the good executive develops know-how, intuition, feel, or common sense which guides him in his executive functions. In fact, in describing the characteristics of good executives Barnard plays down the importance of purely intellectual qualities, feeling that its importance has been overemphasized. Barnard observed, " . . . we know that many very able, intelligent, and learned persons have neither understanding nor correct intuitions about concrete organizations."[36] To be a successful executive involves "taking everything into account," sensing the whole, having a feel of the organization.

To Barnard, intellect enters into the process of acquiring knowledge, but the executive's use of what he knows is more generally a matter of habitual, intuitive response. It is largely a matter of course and, what is more important, it has to be so if it is to be effective. Self-consciousness in much of the executive's action would tend to inhibit speed, accuracy, and forcefulness.

Barnard's emphasis on the nonintellectual aspects of decision processes and leadership shows his pragmatic approach and his objection to the intellectual snobbishness of our society. The main point which he emphasized is that "intellectual competency is *not* a substitute" for characteristics such as vitality, endurance, decisiveness, persuasiveness, and responsibility.[37]

---

[36]*Organization and Management*, p. 90.

[37]*Ibid.*, p. 98. Emphasis in original. Barnard presents this point of view in his article "The Nature of Leadership" reprinted in *Ibid.*, pp. 80–110.

In 1936 Barnard gave a lecture entitled "Mind in Everyday Affairs," to the Engineering Faculty and Students of Princeton University.[38] In this lecture he emphasized the limitation of purely logical, rational decision making and the pervasiveness of what he identified as nonlogical thought processes.[39] Barnard identified logical thought processes as those involving conscious thinking which can be expressed in words or symbols. In contrast, nonlogical thought processes are those not capable of being expressed in words.[40] In his analysis Barnard points out that all too often the executive has to reach a conclusion or make a decision by a specific date and frequently he must do this whether or not he has sufficient data and adequate knowledge. Under such circumstances the executive relies on judgment, hunch, and intuition. He uses nonlogical thought processes, although he seldom admits publicly or even to himself that he is functioning in this manner. Rather, he rationalizes his actions after the act. In other words, the executive frequently acts first and "thinks" (that is, rationalizes) later. Barnard's emphasis on the nonlogical aspect of personal decisions poses a conflict between logical and nonlogical thought processes in organizational decisions. Barnard attempts to resolve this difference by stating that people are split personalities. They have both a personal and an organizational personality. Thus, organizational decisions are made where organizational needs predominate and the personal needs are relegated to a minor level. In short, Barnard maintains that " . . . a sort of a dual personality is required of individuals contributing to organization action — the private personality, and the organization personality."[41]

This differentiation helps the student to understand why Barnard maintains that organizational decisions are more logical than personal decisions. For example, design of formal organization involves establishment of a logical decision-making structure. Barnard's discussions of executive behavior, however, emphasize the nonlogical aspects of decision; thus, in discussing incentives he emphasizes persuasion and points out that it involves nonlogical behavior. Similarly, authority has a subjective aspect and the informal organization itself is personal and not consciously planned. Experience reveals that much executive thinking is subconscious; it involves the feeling mind that senses the end result. This perspective is illus-

---

[38]Reprinted in *The Functions,* pp. 301–322.

[39]*Ibid.,* pp. 301–302.

[40]Barnard's terminology is confusing because it makes the crucial difference between logical and nonlogical thought processes not a question of logic at all, rather it makes the difference rest on the degree to which the individual is consciously aware of his logic. It would be simpler to think of this dichotomy as conscious and nonconscious logic. Intuitive decisions can be and often are correct (that is, they are logical) even though the logic underlying them is not known.

[41]*The Functions,* p. 188.

trated by Barnard's recollection of his own decision-making processes when he built the New Jersey Bell Telephone Company:

> I think under those conditions the confident and ambitious young man makes the right kind of immediate decision without too much reference to the future which he doesn't understand; he doesn't even know there is a future. If he has the *right intuition* about the thing he begins to develop and unroll and he keeps it a tradition. Often the tradition lasts too long and it isn't good; but — Yes! *That's the way the thinking is done, not by sitting down and calculating a whole future of the institution.* I don't think at that time anybody at the top of the organization had a very clear idea of the future of the company.[42]

The consistency of Barnard's opinion as to the importance of nonlogical thought processes is revealed by his impression of the proper role of the laboratory approach to the study of organization behavior. In 1961 he stated his beliefs as follows:

> . . . I think that laboratory work, experimentation, controlled observation, is an important sector of the scientific process, but I think it quite insufficient for scientific development; I think that is demonstrated in the physical field. The quantum theory was developed by a man who had a good deal of laboratory experience, but it didn't come out of that experience. . . .

> . . . You can find many illustrations where very fundamental developments have been foreshadowed by theories that were not based in any definite and concrete way on observations. I would say that was true of the theory of relativity and it was very much true of the development of electrical theory. . . .

> . . . No one has yet explained the power of induction. There's a gap between what you know and what you have observed, so that you jump from here to there. Most of the jumping is bad, it doesn't turn out; nevertheless, that which does turn out was based on that kind of unexplainable jumping in the human mind, something internal which strikes me as a most elusive thing! How did Mozart as a boy write beautiful music? It didn't come from outside instruction. It didn't come from any scholarly study. It came from inside. It's a sense of harmony and relevancy and all that sort of thing. It seems to belong to some people and to be completely absent for others. Now, there are some theorists, and probably more today than there were, especially in mathematical physics and mathematics, who are without practical experience except for the lead pencil and paper; but, generally speaking, the people who can

---

[42]*Conversations*, p. 7. Emphasis added.

produce are those who can add to the effect of intuitive familiarity an analytical approach.[43]

The emphasis on intuition and nonlogical processes leads to concern for the role of intellectual training in developing executive skills. With respect to this Barnard observed:

> I would say that a prerequisite to effective training was a familiarity with the subject matter, a familiarity that was based upon interests and not upon analysis. How do you teach people to write good English? Well, that's the kind of a question you are asking, how do you teach people to write good English? Well, I don't think there is any doubt that there's some point in having instructions in the subject, but I think there's a lot of doubt as to how effective that can be as to the great majority of students. They get something out of it but not the thing you are trying to teach them.[44]

Barnard illustrated this point by recalling his experience as a pianist.

> . . . I had a young friend who was working for a concern that made tape recorders. . . . He was in Boston on a Thanksgiving time when I was up there, and he got me to come over to a studio to record some piano music. Well, it was a beautiful studio, with very little reverberation in it, soundproofed, the piano in perfect tune. I sat down and began to improvise, not knowing that I was being recorded; thought I wasn't. The thing that always interested me about that was the number of things, particularly regarding counterpoint, that I was not conscious of when playing, but which were evident in the final results. On other occasions I've been conscious of the same thing. It applies to management and everything else that I can think of. No one would claim that there was no point in having instructions in piano. There are technical accomplishments that have to be acquired; but, except for the really highest performances, some very first class amateurs — some of whom are absolutely illiterate — can produce very excellent results. When I worked in the piano factory there was a rather low-grade fellow who did some work around there, I don't know what it was; but he also taught dancing and he played the piano. He couldn't read a note. It was all improvised and it was darned good; he was really good![45]

The problem of studying decision making is thus involved with the study of thought processes, and it is evident that both logical and nonlogical processes enter into decisions. The difference between organizational and personal decisions is significant. Organizational decisions tend to be more

---

[43]*Ibid.*, pp. 19–20.
[44]*Ibid.*, pp. 20–21.
[45]*Ibid.*, p. 21.

logical than personal decisions because goals are explicitly stated and reasons for action have been communicated to others. It is extremely difficult, however, to separate personal needs from behavior even when one is performing in an organizational role.

By viewing the individual as having a private personality and an organizational personality, Barnard can deal with organizational decisions as separate from the private decisions of individuals. In fact, in *The Functions of the Executive* he defines "decision" as the acts of individuals which are the result of deliberation, calculation, and thought. He sees decision making as a logical process of discrimination, analysis, and choice.[46] By definition Barnard thus eliminates the problem posed by the concept of nonlogical thought processes. Such nonlogical processes are unconscious and responsive, the results of present or past internal or external conditions. Barnard explains this concept of organization decision:

> The acts of organizations are those of persons dominated by organizational, not personal, ends. These ends, especially those which are most general or remote, since they represent a concensus of opinion, may be arrived at by non-logical processes; but since they must usually be formulated in some degree, whereas individual ends more rarely need to be formulated, the ends of organization to a relatively high degree involve logical processes, not as rationalizations after decision but as processes of decision. Moreover, when ends have been adopted, the coordination of acts as means to these ends is itself an essentially logical process. The discrimination of facts and the allocation of acts by specialization which coordination implies may quite appropriately be regarded as logical or deliberate thinking processes of organization, though not necessarily logical processes of thought of the individual participants. Generally, however, it will be observed that the more important *organization* acts of individuals are likely also to be logical — in that they require deliberate choice of means to accomplish ends which are not personal, and therefore cannot be directly automatic or responsive reactions.

> This does not mean that unconscious, automatic, responsive, action is not involved in organization. On the contrary, the discussion of informal organization . . . has suggested that non-logical organization processes are indispensible to formal organization. Moreover, much of the action of individuals participating in organization is habitual, repetitive, and may be merely responsive by *organization design* — a result, for example, of specialization intended to enhance this non-logical process. What is important here, however, is the superlative degree to which logical processes must and can characterize organization action as

---

[46]*The Functions*, p. 185.

contrasted with individual action, and the degree to which decision is specialized in organization. It is the deliberate adoption of means to ends which is the essence of formal organization.[47]

Obviously, Barnard sees the nonlogical aspects of human behavior as being modified when they are dominated by organizational ends. It must be recognized, however, that this is a matter of degree and that, according to Barnard, the successful executive has to perfect the fine art of decision making. He senses the whole. He intuitively or subconsciously takes into consideration a wide complexity of dynamic factors which he cannot simultaneously consciously comprehend. This point of view was held by Barnard shortly before his death. For example, when asked his opinion of the mathematical-computer or management-science approach to business management, Barnard commented:

> . . . it may prove useful when sufficiently developed and when its limitations are also thoroughly understood. I would say in the field of aeronautics and modern electricity that there's a good deal that could not ever have been attained by intuitive familiarity. Particularly in the case of airplanes, there is very much that has been dependent upon pure mathematical calculation that would be outside the range of the ordinary human capacity to dope out; *but you couldn't run an airplane industry on it.* While I think that the mathematical model method of Simon's may prove useful in an intellectual sense, *I yet have to be shown that it will enable men effectively to put the whole picture together, which is what you have to do in a running stream of events.*
>
> You have to assume a too static world to operate in some of these techniques.[48]

The Environment of Decision Making

Despite Barnard's continued reiteration of the importance of nonlogical thought processes and his concern over the erroneous assumption that conscious reasoning can and should always guide what we do, these concepts have had slight impact on present day management theory. In contrast his ideas on the study of organizational decision-making processes as logical acts have had widespread influence. A review of the current literature reveals that such Barnardian concepts as the importance of knowing when not to decide, the process of composite decision, and delineation of strategic factors in decisions have had wide acceptability and considerable impact.[49]

---

[47]*Ibid.*, pp. 185–186.
[48]*Conversations*, p. 22. Emphasis added.
[49]For example, see William J. Gore and Fred S. Selander, "Research Notes and Comments: A Bibliographical Essay on Decision Making," *Administrative Science Quarterly*

Barnard discusses decisions by differentiating between decisions as to ends and as to means and between personal decisions and organization decisions.

Decisions on goals, purposes, or ends are dominated by the moral element (what ought to be). Whereas decisions as to means toward ends tend to be dominated by opportunistic elements, with how one can deal with an existing environment in order to achieve stated ends. The difference between decisions as to means and those as to ends is not a clear-cut, precise matter, for the end itself may be a means toward a broader and more remote end.

Personal Decisions and Organizational Decisions

There are five significant differences between an individual's personal decisions and those he makes in his organizational role. First, organizational decisions are impersonal and are dominated by organizational ends. Organizational goals or purposes are formulated in an explicit manner, whereas this need not be so for personal decisions. Third, the ends of organization are usually arrived at by a high degree of logical and involved processes, whereas the individual may arrive at personal ends through subconscious processes involving sentiments and conditioning by his earlier environment. Logical processes characterize organization actions as contrasted with individual actions. Personal decisions can't be delegated to others; organizational decisions not only can be delegated, but usually are. Last, organizational decisions are specialized; personal decisions are not specialized. Thus we see that organizational decisions are characterized by a high degree of specialization and by logical processes. They are one of the ties that binds the organization into a concrete system of coordinated parts.

It is important to differentiate between organizational and personal decisions. The personal decision in organization is a function of incentives and acceptance of authority. Its essence is willingness to cooperate or participate and it is thus a matter of subjective choice. Organizational decisions are those made with organization purposes or goals in mind. They are basically impersonal and organizational in intent and effect.

---

4 (June 1959): 97–121; and Simon, *Administrative Behavior*, pp. 1, 12, 55, 133, 203, 204, 221. Simon observed, "Even Barnard, whose critical insight usually saves him from the 'practical man' fallacy, credits the intuitional faculties with considerable more validity than seems to be due them" (p. 190). See also Robert Tannenbaum, "Management Decision Making," *Journal of Business* 23 (January 1950): 22; Norman H. Martin, "Differential Decisions in the Management of an Industrial Plant," *Journal of Business* 29 (October 1956): 249; Dickson Reck, "The Role of Company Standards in Industrial Administration," *Advanced Management* 19 (April 1954): 19–23; and George A. Steiner, "How to Forecast Defense Expenditure," *California Management Review* 3 (Summer 1960): 92.

The Occasions for Decisions in Organizations

The first thing to say about the making of decisions in organizations is that men generally try to avoid decisions and, in the process, they overlook the fact that a decision not to decide is a decision with all of its consequences. Much decision making involves "finding a reason why something should not be done." Thus, "The processes of decision . . . are largely techniques for narrowing choice."[50]

The second thing to observe is that the character of decisions tends to change as one moves down the executive hierarchy. At the upper limits decisions regarding purpose or goals receive major attention and those relating to means are secondary. This proportion tends to shift and reverse itself as one moves down the hierarchy of organization because the executive position within an organization is consciously designed to limit both the executive's obligation to make decisions and the area in which he is to make them.

A job definition describes the parameters of executive jurisdiction, but not with precision. The interpretation of the definition involves decisions as to how far, on what, and when the executive should act. Usually the occasions for decisions aid, in part, in deciding these questions, for executives may be called upon to make decisions at the instigation of superiors, at the urging of subordinates, or on their own initiative. Decisions made on the executive's own initiative are probably the most important to this discussion for they involve not only deciding but also justifying the decision to others in the organization. When an executive decides on his own there is always a question of the necessity of the decision as well as its scope. The decision is, thus, generally reviewed by superiors in the organization and this review, in turn, puts the onus for justifying the decision upon the decision maker.

Most of the above is concerned with executive decisions. What is overlooked is the fact that the decisions of nonexecutive participants in the organization are significant. Theirs are the on-the-spot decisions which bring about coordinated activities. The executive decisions simply set limits and suggest methods so that the choices are clear and comprehensible.

Evaluation of Executive Decisions

One of the great difficulties in judging executives is that many of their significant decisions are difficult to observe and even more difficult to evaluate. Many are decisions not to decide; many are decisions regarding what to do, but involve a complex chain of orders to attempt achievement;

---

[50]*The Functions*, p. 14.

and still others are decisions which involve a conscious decision to delay communication. It follows that if something cannot be measured or observed it cannot be directly evaluated.

The Opportunistic Element in Decision Making

A starting place for the discussion of opportunistic elements in decision making is to reconstruct the general theory of organization which Barnard evolved, namely, that a formal organization is a cooperative system consisting of the coordinated activities of two or more persons. Barnard emphasized the role of informal organization, the general nature of systems (for example, the problems implicit in the systems concept such as the parts and the whole, the fallacy of composition, a change in one part changing the whole, and so forth), the nature of persons as individuals contrasted with their activities within the cooperative system, and the concept of purpose as the unifying element in an organization.

With respect to formal organization Barnard noted that complex organization is made up of unit organizations and that the problems of communication that are associated with the increasing complexity of organizations give rise to an executive organization. Executives, by simultaneously acting as members of their unit organizations and of the executive organization, contribute to the organic unity of the whole.

His analysis noted that incentives and authority are part of the development of the will to cooperate as well as aspects of coordination. In discussing the decision-making process many of the observations previously made were reviewed. The process is the device by which coordination is obtained. Through it successive levels in the hierarchy establish or decide upon their actions regarding more broadly stated purposes. Decisions at the top of the organizational hierarchy are transmitted and translated as they descend to the lower levels. In the process the emphasis tends to shift from purposes to means. The process of sequential decision making in the hierarchy of organization is important to both coordination of the parts and maintainence of the sense of organic whole for the organization.

The opportunistic element in decision making is concerned with short-run decisions, what might be conveniently thought of as the decisions of adjusting means to reach stated ends. " . . . in most cases the ends of organization action are the unique results of the *action* of organization itself."[51] They usually are based on the concept of the good of the organization where "good" refers to the relation of the organization to its participants or to the general environment. Moreover, the good of the organization always refers to the future and the nature of ends involves the moral

---

[51]*Ibid.*, p. 200. Emphasis in original.

element in decision making. Since formal organization cannot act without purpose or purposes it is evident that the moral element is always present. What are appropriate ends is a significant moral question.

When we focus upon the opportunistic element in decision making we are taking a short-run view and considering that for practical purposes ends are established. This view involves analysis of existing circumstances with reference to purpose: What are the means for achieving the stated ends?

For decision making based upon analysis of existing factors in relation to a purpose Barnard presents a concept which he calls "the theory of the strategic factor." In essence the theory is an exercise using the system concept. Simply stated it holds that a system is an organic whole. It is the result of the interactions of its parts with each other and the whole. The parts, however, can be identified as limiting factors, "those which if absent or changed would accomplish the desired purpose, provided the others remained unchanged," and complementary factors, those that would have to remain unchanged. In fact, "a limiting strategic factor is the one whose control, in the right form at the right place and time, will establish a new system . . . which meets the purpose."[52]

Barnard chose the word "strategic" over "limiting" in order to interject the dynamic element of the relatively changing position of the decision maker. His decision interacts with the field (organization) in which it is developed and thus something new evolves.

The opportunistic element in decision making involves discrimination of strategic factors (that is, analysis) which, when established, reduces purpose to a new and more precise objective.

The organizational decision-making process requires a sequence of decisions at different times and by different executives and other persons in different positions. "A broad purpose and a broad decision require fragmentation of purpose into detailed purposes and of principal general decisions into subsidiary decisions."[53] These need to be made in proper sequence so that the decision-making process becomes one of successive opportunities leading to further refinement of purpose.

The discrimination of strategic factors varies with the nature of the environment being considered. One can view it as being increasingly difficult to discriminate as one moves from physical to chemical to biological to physiological to psychological to economic to political to social to moral elements. The available technologies help significantly at the hard-science end of the continuum, for example, physics and chemistry. As we approach the social sciences and morals, however, there tends to be confusion and

---

[52]*Ibid.*, p. 203.
[53]*Ibid.*, p. 206.

error. One common error is to confuse the past with the present. The legitimate significance of the past is in the understanding it helps develop as a basis for redefining purpose; it aids in judging future consequences.

Finally, opportunism in decision making is the aspect which involves means to ends; as such it also involves logical analytical processes, experiment and observation, and specialization. (It is in this aspect of decision making that the power of cooperation is most apparent.) Although decision making involves analysis it must be viewed as a synthesis. "The background out of which strategic factors are analyzed is the whole situation to which the decision relates."[54] The analysis is not the end but the beginning of purposive action. In other words, we must remember that an organization is a system, the parts cannot be separated out; the organization cannot be reified if it is studied in terms of its parts. It must be recognized that the characteristics of each part and aspect are determined by the total organization and at the same time each interacts with the whole and its parts to determine the nature of the total organization.

Status Systems

An important aspect of Barnard's conceptualization of the general nature of organization is his recognition of the characteristics of status systems and of the fact that status is systematic and, to a considerable degree, independent of structural aspects of organization. (Status is necessarily systematized in formal organization.) Status systems are intimately tied to other essential features of organization such as communication, authority, and incentive; moreover, their function of providing incentive tends to link them to the broader society in which the organization exists. Status, thus, is related to the value system of society as well as to the internal life of the organization.[55]

Barnard holds that status systems are necessary from the point of view of individuals as well as that of the formal cooperative system. He goes further and observes that status systems tend to become rigid and to spread so that ultimately they weaken or destroy the organization.

As referred to above, status has a specific meaning. It is defined organizationally with reference to specific individuals and, in essence, consists

---

[54]*Ibid.*, p. 239 fn.

[55]Barnard failed to discuss status systems in *The Functions of the Executive*. As he stated, "I had left out of my book if not Hamlet, perhaps Ophelia, and did not discover it for seven years. . . ." (*Organization and Management,* p. xi). In August 1945 Barnard gave a lecture at the University of Chicago titled "Functions and Pathology of Status Systems in Formal Organizations." This lecture was reprinted in *Industry and Society,* William F. Whyte, ed. (New York: McGraw Hill, 1946) and in *Organization and Management,* pp. 207–244.

of the rights, privileges, duties, and obligations of an individual within an organization. Status tends to establish important aspects of the behavior of individuals and, in so doing, develops organization members' expectations regarding the way members with certain assigned statuses will behave.

Status becomes systematic in an organization by codification of the symbols and the common connotation given to such symbols. Titles, insignia, and location of work, thus, become symbolic of status positions of individuals within organizations.

Functional Status Systems and Scalar Status Systems

The systems of status found in organizations are interdependent and overlap. Despite this Barnard identifies two fairly distinct types: systems of status arising out of functions performed and systems of status arising out of the organizational hierarchy and involving formal authority and jurisdiction of formally assigned responsibility.

The first of these, called functional status, is usually related to horizontal division of labor; and thus it is a general attribute of a craft or profession. For example, a carpenter is given certain rights and privileges and assumes certain obligations on the basis of his craft. If one is told that a specific worker is a carpenter the rights, duties, privileges, and obligations associated with the function of carpentry become established for that particular carpenter in the context of the specific organization to which he is contributing his service.

The second kind of status, scalar status, is determined by the superiority or subordination relation and is identified in terms of formal authority and formal responsibility or jurisdiction.[56]

Devices Used by Organizations to Establish Status

The general ideas underlying Barnard's discussion of status can be illustrated by pointing to some of the more common methods used to establish and maintain status systems. These are the use of ceremonies in relation to indoctrination of new members or new office holders; the use of special insignia such as uniforms, medals, ties and pins; titles of address; privileges of office such as the use of a company automobile, a private secretary, a private office; and code of conduct for those within a specific system of states. Accepted rules of behavior also tend to maintain some

---

[56]Although Barnard omits it, a third kind of status should be recognized. Informal status is related to personal characteristics of individuals and may be distinct and different from formally identified status. Compare Melville Dalton, *Men Who Manage* (New York: John Wiley, 1958).

of the status differentials, for example, in the military an officer is expected to refrain from fraternizing with his men.

The Functions of Status Systems

Practically all formal organizations develop status systems which serve the needs of individuals as well as those of organizations. Symbols of status have the effect of credentials. They serve as introductions which identify individual roles and abilities. Thus, titles signify, in a tentative way, the social role of the individual within an organization. Such titles are necessary tools to allow the individual to do his work. In two ways status systems provide devices for protecting the integrity of the individual in a social environment. They endorse a person's past history, that is they grant evidence of attainment. (This is anointment, not reward.) Without such endorsement the individual might not consider the effort he puts into his self-development worthwhile. For example, the earning of a Ph.D. grants permanent status to the individual. Status systems also satisfy those of higher formal authority so that orders will be accepted. It involves a loss of self-respect to receive orders from a nondescript somebody. "Men are eager to be 'bossed' by superior ability but they resent being bossed by men of no greater ability than they themselves have."[57] Men want to believe that those in higher authority know what they are doing. This knowledge is difficult to establish by absolute criteria and thus, to a degree, status gives an aura of acceptability to higher level positions. Similarly, there is a tendency for functional status to imply competence, and authorization to act tends to be granted to those with functional status. Still a third way status systems preserve personal integrity is by preserving the integrity of the organization; "to be a member of a good organization is a personal asset."[58] Office becomes symbolic of the organization and the top official, in his person, tends to signify the organization. Finally, status systems provide means for recognizing individual differences and for protecting individuals from direct comparisons of abilities that are in fact unequal. " . . . where differences of status are recognized formally, men of unequal abilities and importance can and do work together well for long periods."[59]

From the point of view of the organization status systems contribute to the functions of coordinating behavior, that is, to the maintenance of the cooperative system. In fact, a great deal of the executive's work involves maintaining and changing status systems, for example, changing the for-

---

[57]*Organization and Management*, p. 220.
[58]*Ibid.*, p. 221.
[59]*Ibid.*, p. 223.

mal structure of the hierarchy, selecting and placing personnel, carrying on official ceremonies, and so forth.

Barnard sees status systems as formal means for recognizing and dealing with differences between individual abilities, jobs, and contributions to the organization. Moreover, status systems provide a system of organization communication. They tend to insure that communications are authoritative, authentic, and intelligible. Those who have status are presumed to have the right and to possess the authority to make decisions within their specialized areas. Moreover, in scalar status authority is related to being at a communication center and involves translation of language into proper levels for each status group. Systems of status are thus indispensable guides to the selection of the appropriate language which insures that messages are intelligible.

Status systems contribute to organizational effectiveness in additional ways. They provide incentives to individuals by providing prestige which is frequently valued individually, as well as a means for obtaining other ends. They also are an indispensable developer of the sense of responsibility and, therefore, contribute to reliability and stability. This aspect arises from the seriousness to the individual of loss of status. People behave responsibly in order to improve their status or to protect it.

Disruptive Tendencies in Status Systems

Although status systems are essential to formal organizations, they also release disruptive tendencies. An important aspect of the executive's work is to counteract the possible negative impact of status systems upon the cooperative system.

The disruptive or pathological aspects of status systems can be summarized as follows:

1. They tend to give a distorted value to individuals. Status systems arise because of individual differences in ability, skills, training, the value of work performed, and importance to the system of communication. Thus, status may be assigned for a variety of reasons of which only one (individual differences in ability) is correlated with the commonly held value that a person should be judged on his own merits. Thus, the status given to a specific individual may be distorted and unrelated to his personal worth.

2. Status systems require some stability, a requirement which in turn causes harmful rigidities in the cooperative system. If a status system is to serve as an effective incentive, status must be stable. Individuals want some assurance that they will retain achieved status. Similarly, it appears that individuals are more concerned with avoiding loss of status than they

are with achieving higher status. Finally, good communications tend to be broken down by frequent changes in status relations. Thus the requirement of stability tends to cause rigidities that limit frequent change, inhibit the circulation of men of outstanding ability, cause those of declining ability to be kept in jobs for which they are inadequate, and limit redefinition of positions to adjust for changing environmental needs.

3. Status systems may set up "unjust" differentials in rewards and may thwart commonly held concepts of distributive justice. The injustices develop from excessive rewards for higher status and lack of freedom to promote or demote to insure that higher-status individuals are automatically those of higher ability.

4. Status systems tend to detract from morale by exaggerating the needs of administration. This problem arises from the fact that an effective system of communication requires habitual practices and technical procedures. "The lines of communication, the system of status, and the associated procedures . . . are essential tools of administration and are the most 'visible' general parts of it."[60] Being tangible these tend to be viewed as the *sine qua non* of the organization. They tend to inhibit changes in status and to prevent abler men being promoted. Moreover, they tend to put a premium upon following routines and doing things in the accepted manner.

5. Finally, status systems tend to limit the adaptability of an organization because the symbolism which gives status to holders of official positions tends to transfer the status of the office to the individual. The individual becomes symbolic of the organization. When this happens it is difficult to remove the individual from his official position even if his capacities are not up to the job. Thus, the organization's adaptability to changing conditions is limited by the capabilities of its top executive who has come to symbolize the organization.

In summary, the status systems in an organization are essential to its effectiveness. At the same time they lead to rigidity and inflexibility. The systems present the executive with serious problems, complicated by the fact that his position is dependent upon a status system. These problems center on the needs to insure correspondence between status and ability (which requires free movements of personnel); to prevent systems of status from becoming ends in themselves or primary means; and to see that the rewards of office or position are proportionate to the necessary level of incentives and morale.

To mitigate, if not solve, these problems requires great ability and extraordinary moral courage.

---

[60]*Ibid.*, p. 240.

Organizational Morals[61]

An important aspect of organization is the fact that every formal organization is a social system. As such each develops and gives expression to beliefs, convictions, mores, and patterns of culture which make it a largely autonomous moral institution. Thus, cooperation among men, through formal organization, creates moralities and these moralities may have little or no reference to broader society's prevalent moral concepts.

In discussing organization morality Barnard emphasizes the following: organization morality tends to be autonomous and distinct from morality of the broader society; it tends to be complex and to involve varying codes which may be, and often are, contradictory; and it is an important part of executive functions because many management decisions are concerned with moral issues.

Morality Defined

As used here morality or moral behavior is "that which is governed by beliefs or feelings of what is right or wrong regardless of self-interest or immediate consequences of a decision to do or not to do specific things under particular conditions."[62]

In business such codes of conduct are seldom viewed as "moral." Instead they are referred to as loyalty, responsibility, duties, and the like. These euphemisms, however, involve morality and the feelings of guilt, remorse, and anxiety when a code is violated.

Varieties in Business Morality Codes

The moralities of business are complex and contradictory. In any organization three codes tend to operate: individual personal codes of right behavior such as charity, humility, honesty, and respect for the rights of others; organizational codes regarding the good of the organization; and codes regarding the good of society. What adds to the difficulty in discussing organization morality is the fact that the moral climate in each organization is unique, for example, there are differences in the concepts of responsibility and loyalty when one compares a hospital, a telephone company, and a shirt plant. For purpose of discussion two responsibilities are found within organizations, personal and representative or official responsibilities.

Personal responsibilities are personally held values arising from the

---

[61]This treatment of organization morals is based primarily on Barnard's article "Elementary Conditions of Business Morals," *California Management Review* 1 (Fall 1958): 1–13.

[62]*Ibid.,* p. 4.

ethics of the individual. They are part of his character and are related to the environment in which he developed. They deal with such things as honesty, reliability, respect for the rights of others, the honor of his word when given, and so forth.

Representative or official responsibilities arise when the behavior of an individual in a formal organization becomes representative rather than personal. The individual then acts on behalf of his role or the organization or both, rather than on behalf of himself. His action "is in accordance with aims or goals or by methods determined by others."[63] There is a wide gap between personal ethics and representative ethics. For example, the behavior of an individual acting as a trustee of an estate is prescribed by the legal and moral codes that are divorced from direct personal interest. Ethics of personal behavior are not identical with those of representative behavior. At times it is moral from the standpoint of representative behavior to do things that are immoral from the personal point of view, and often there is conflict between moralities.

Representative behavior is the basis upon which a complex structure of moralities is erected in formal organizations. The following are some of these moralities.

Personnel loyalties resemble personal loyalties, but in fact they are quite different. Personnel loyalties involve "loyalties to individuals acting in their official capacities. Loyalty in this context means recognition of the responsibilities of others and the desire to support others in the discharge of those responsibilities."[64] They are important to the cohesiveness of organizations, but they are not the same thing as personal loyalties. In fact personnel loyalties tend to change as soon as job responsibilities change. It is the exception when two persons maintain a close personal friendship after their official relation is significantly altered, for example, by promotion or retirement.

Corporate responsibilities are involved when the trustees, officers, and employees of organizations by their actions give credence to the myth that the organization is a fictitious person. Their decisions impute a moral responsibility which is different from personal morality or official organization morality and which is in many respects irrelevant to these. The responsibilities of corporations are of two kinds: those relating to the balancing of interests between stockholders, creditors, directors, officers, and employees and those relating to competitors, government, local communities, and society in general.

Organizational loyalties are distinct from corporate responsibilities. In some situations there is a distinction between the corporate entity and

---

[63]*Ibid.*, p. 6.
[64]*Ibid.*

organizations, but in general the two are similar. Many individuals feel an obligation to the organization and the personal sacrifices for the good of the organization represent a high type of moral character. Such morality tends to develop after a person becomes attached to an organization.

Economic responsibility is frequently overlooked. It involves avoiding waste, debts, and inefficiency.

Technical and technological responsibility is found especially in the creative artist, the scientist, and the artisan who have a morality regarding how work should be performed. Standards of workmanship are involved and it is evident that most individuals adhere to standards of quality and quantity that involve moral factors.

Legal responsibility is yet another kind of morality encountered in organization. It involves a propensity to conform to legal edicts and belief in the importance of upholding rules and regulations.

The above represent a cursory summary of Barnard's treatment of the kinds of morality involved in business organizations. The point of it is that moral factors are of predominant importance. They are complex and involve many contradictions. One can expect conflict of responsibilities to be characteristic of cooperative effort. At present, too little is known about this aspect of organization.

Summary

The preceding presents the essence of Chester I. Barnard's ideas about organization. The central theme is that executive functions have to be visualized within the broader concept of the organization. In final analysis, executive functions are specialized activities designed to perpetuate and maintain the organization. Thus, what is covered is an attempt to conceptualize in a general way the nature of organizations.

Much of what is dealt with can be integrated as a matter of analytical reasoning. If one proceeds from Barnard's definition to his analysis he can see the logical relations between the subjects of this discourse. Thus, the first proposition is that an organization is a system of consciously coordinated activities of two or more persons. This proposition immediately implies some inferences: An organization is a system; therefore, the general properties of systems apply to it. An organization consists of the consciously coordinated activities of persons. It, therefore, follows that there is purpose which is the unifying concept underlying and implicit in coordination of activities, there is communication which is the *sine qua non* of conscious coordination; there are people; and the people can and will cooperate.

The discussion has considered each of these in turn. For example, looking at organizations in the context of systems theory we see that:

1. They are complex. Each part is at the same time a determined and determining force or factor in the system.

2. Simple cause-and-effect reasoning is not applicable. To change one part is to change relations to other parts and in effect to change the characteristics of the system. Thus, the system is dealt with by trying to manipulate factors of strategic importance in the system. It should be recognized, however, that the system as a whole is more than the sum of its parts.

3. The organization as a system exists in the context of broader systems such as the institutional framework of society. Hence, in a sense it is part of a broader system and realistically it should be seen in relation to the broader environment. For purpose of study, however, we can artificially separate out specific organizations.

The above remarks flow directly from the definitions. The observation that the cooperative system is concerned with people leads us into discussions of seven topics:

1. The nature of people involves free will and determinism, and the problems of individuals in organization roles contrasted with individuals as integrated personalities.

2. Consideration of the nature of people leads to consideration of the nonplanned aspects of organizations, what Barnard identified as informal organization. Informal organization is one of the strong forces of social control in formal organization.

3. Consideration of incentives involves ways of developing the willingness to cooperate.

4. Consideration of the nature of authority and its functions within organization relates to maintaining willingness to contribute effort as well as to maintaining the communication necessary for cooperative effort.

5. Decision making is the process of determining purpose or redefining purpose as well as that of attaining ends with available means. The role of strategic factors is of great relevance. In addition, the concept of the organization as a dynamic system leads to recognition of the need by decision makers to have a feel for the whole to which the decision relates.

6. Status systems involve recognition of the fact that organizations are composed of individuals of differing abilities (aptitudes). When individuals are working on jobs of varying importance to the organization and effective communication between the parts of the organization is required then the manner in which organizations integrate such differences and maintain the system of communication must be considered. This involves analysis of status systems as the means for maintaining authority, developing in-

centives, facilitating communication, and maintaining the integrity of individual responsibility.

7. Organization morals are involved in the conflict of personal versus organizational ends which has been implicit in much of our analysis. The nature of the moral elements in organization are seen to be of predominant importance to understanding the dynamics of organizational life.

VI.

The Functions of the Executive

Barnard's treatment of executive functions is a natural outgrowth of his theory of formal organization and his analysis of the elements of organization. He sees the executive organization as essential to formal centers where communications come together. These centers are occupied by those performing executive functions. Moreover, for an organization to be effective personnel must be able and willing to contribute to organizational activities and there must be purpose or goals to guide activity. To Barnard these are the executive functions. He identifies them as providing the system of organizational communication, securing essential efforts, and formulating and defining purpose.

These are interrelated and interdependent aspects of maintaining the organization; hence, it should be recognized that the threefold classification system is arbitrary. One function automatically implies the other and in actual practice they cannot be separated from each other.

Providing the Organizational Communication System

Communication is a *sine qua non* for complex formal organization. The parts have to be related to the whole, purposes need to be identified and accepted, and the proper sequence of events needs to be maintained. These actions all involve communication and, as Barnard emphasized, the complexity of formal organization establishes the need for, or the *raison d'etre* of, a formal system of communication, namely, the executive organization. The system of communication in the executive organization involves establishing or defining executive jobs and securing persons capable of filling such jobs. These problems are interrelated and in actual practice one sees that executive jobs are defined and modified in accordance with the potential of the available personnel. Moreover, they are redefined again in terms of the changing needs of the whole organization which is constantly adjusting to both internal and external forces. The executive system, its nerve center, is the primary agent for sensing the need to adjust and for initiating the needed action; hence, an important problem of the executive organization is that of obtaining the coalescence of executive personnel and executive position.

The Scheme of Organization

The problem of formally defining executive positions is essentially that of the design of the formal organizational structure. As such its solution is influenced by the general factors involved in specialization and division of labor, for example, location, time sequence, task, technology, and the compatibility of people.

The scheme of organization is frequently treated as an independent variable in the general framework of organization, a tendency encouraged by the fact that it is relatively easily portrayed in terms of organization charts and job descriptions. What tends to be overlooked is that the scheme of organization is an interdependent factor in the total field of the organization. That the scheme exists in a system of mutual causality must be recognized as well as that it is only a rough approximation and presents no more than a crude skeleton of the functioning organization.

What gives the scheme of the executive organization life and vitality is the informal executive organization. Barnard's analysis tends to follow the framework he used in dealing with organization in general,[1] namely, that executive organization has both formal and informal dimensions. Barnard tends to emphasize the importance of the informal organization in facilitating communication and preserving the general organization. His reasoning centers on the need for communication within the executive organization, and the development of communication through mutual trust and personal understanding. Barnard concludes that an important aspect of the informal organization is to insure that the persons composing it are socially compatible, regardless of their competence. This compatibility involves feeling comfortable and having rapport. Generally it is a function of such things as cultural background, age, religion, political orientation, race, education, and values as well as personal appearance and modes of behavior.[2]

The informal organization and the personal compatibility upon which this organization is based is promoted within the organization through rewards and penalties as well as precepts established by the actions of executives and the interaction produced within conferences.

---

[1] See pages 60–72.

[2] In pointing to these factors Barnard is describing the group of assorted prejudices that one encounters in organizations. See, for example, Melville Dalton, *Men Who Manage* (New York: John Wiley, 1958).

Frequently overlooked is the important function of the informal executive organization to provide a method by which opinions, suspicions, and other intangible facts are communicated. These could not pass through formal channels without causing difficulty such as forcing decisions, dissipating objective authority, and overloading executive positions. The objective authority of formal organization will not stand much open division; hence, the informal executive organization lessens such division and keeps it from becoming overt.

Executive Personnel

Barnard sees the securing of executive personnel as special personnel problems with the unique aspects centering on obtaining persons with proper character and ability as well as motivating them to use their capabilities.

It is in describing the qualifications of good executives that Barnard contradicts much commonly encountered speculation as to what it takes to be an executive. In essence Barnard believes that the most important characteristic of the executive is an ability to sense the whole and the harmony of the parts in contributing to the whole; the executive must feel the infinite complexity known as organization. He needs to sense his organization as a whole as well as the total situation relevant to it. He must also have a sense of responsibility that is dominated by the needs of the organization. He must be willing to submit his personal interest to the broader interests of the organization. This characteristic is usually referred to as loyalty to the organization and it is difficult to create. Certainly, material inducements alone will not produce it. Other characteristics the executive should have are flexibility, courage, judgment, alertness, and special training or the aptitudes to learn specific skills.

The formal organization of executive work tends to be significantly influenced by the scarcity of men of general executive ability and the need to keep channels of communication as short as possible. These limitations lead to attempts to keep the number of executives to a minimum and to the use of numerous staff specialists. These staff people supplement the executive's time, energy, and technical capacity. The operation of such executive organizations involves the highest form of executive art. It is evident that man's inability to improve upon and innovate in designing more effective executive organizations is a limitation on the size of complex organization.

The Securing of Essential Services

Barnard's second broad and general executive function is that of securing essential services. He includes in this function the securing of services from suppliers of capital and from customers, an important and generally overlooked aspect of the executive's function.

With respect to the more commonly discussed aspect of securing essential services Barnard observes that it is an important and vital function of the executive to motivate employees. It involves recruiting people who are apt to fit into the organization, motivating and persuading such individuals to contribute their specialized services, and other activities for promoting solidarity, loyalty, quality of output, and compliance with job specifications. The functions of the executive thus include deliberately maintaining and protecting the objective authority of the organization.

The Formulation of Purposes and Objectives

The third executive function emphasized by Barnard is the formulation and definition of organizational purposes. With respect to these he observed that no single executive can accomplish this function by himself. Purpose is defined by action as well as words and the aggregate of actions speaks louder than words. To be effective a purpose must be accepted by all contributors; thus, it must be redefined in terms of specific objectives for specialized units. In essence, what Barnard says is that the critical aspect of formulation of purpose is the assignment of responsibility, that is, the delegation of objective authority so that purposes will be interrelated to coordinate the system as a whole.

It is in Barnard's discussion of purpose that one can perceive what in recent years has become popularly known as management by objective, for what Barnard observes is that there must be an integration and proper sequencing of decisions up and down the chain of formal organization. "Sensitive systems of communication"[3] and delegation of responsibility must allow formulation of grand purposes and their redefinition to purposeful decisions where ultimate effort resides, with the basic units of organization.

These executive functions described above in a general and abstract manner do not exist in isolation. They are merely elements of an organic whole. "It is their combination in a working system that makes an organization."[4]

The Executive Process

Barnard sees executive functions as aspects of organization as a whole. They "have no separate concrete existence."[5] Carrying out executive func-

---

[3]*The Functions*, p. 233.
[4]*Ibid.*, p. 235.
[5]*Ibid.*, p. 235.

tions involves "a sensing of the organization as a whole and the total situation relevant to it."[6] It is more than determining the techniques for attaining effectiveness of specific units. It is a matter of feeling, balance, sense and appropriateness. As such it is a matter of art rather than science. This fact is difficult for many to understand because a complex formal organization breaks up general purpose into detailed tasks. Each task has its respective strategic factors. Thus, it appears that effectiveness of the organization simply requires that each unit should be effective. What this view overlooks is the "dependence of each technical process on all the others used in the same cooperative system."[7]

Barnard sums this up by observing that before an executive acts he needs to know what the side effects are going to be.

> Now every good executive is conscious of [side effects] all of the time; if I do this which I'd like to do, I'll accomplish this result; but in the course of doing it I will produce these other circumstances which may be very much more troublesome and more important. That's the hardest thing to get an amateur to see; *it's the thing that the professional understands with respect to his own profession.*[8]

"Thus the executive process . . . is one of integration of the whole, of finding the effective balance between the local and the broad considerations. . . . "[9] Moreover, the general executive process is not primarily intellectual; "it is aesthetic and moral."[10]

Executive Leadership

The effectiveness of the executive process involves leadership, that is, "the quality of the behavior of individuals whereby they guide people or their activities in organized effort."[11]

Leadership is

> the power of individuals to inspire cooperative personal decision by creating faith: faith in common understanding, faith in the probability of success, faith in the ultimate satisfaction of personal motives, faith in the integrity of objective authority, faith in the superiority of common purpose as a personal aim of those who partake in it.[12]

A significant aspect of leadership is the moral element and it should be

---

[6]*Ibid.*, p. 235.
[7]*Ibid.*, p. 237.
[8]*Conversations*, p. 32. Emphasis added.
[9]*The Functions*, p. 238.
[10]*Ibid.*, p. 257.
[11]*Organization and Management*, p. 83.
[12]*The Functions*, p. 259.

recognized that without leadership and its moral elements organizations do not survive. Without the creation of faith there is no enduring cooperation. Although "cooperation, not leadership, is the creative process . . . leadership is the indispensable fulminator of its forces."[13]

For purposes of discussion Barnard analyzes leadership in terms of two different aspects, technical factors and moral factors. The technical aspects are determined by local considerations (that is, the individual, the followers, and the conditions) and are related to such things as superior ability in specific tasks. Thus, they vary according to time and place. What constitutes technical leadership is determined by the immediate needs of a situation, as well as the training, skill, education, and physical condition of the individual. The point to be emphasized is that the technical aspects of leadership depend upon the local environment in which it is exercised. As such there is little that can be said in a general sense about the technical phases of leadership. On the other hand the moral aspects of leadership are more general and constant and less variable with environmental conditions. Hence, Barnard focuses attention on this particular aspect of leadership.

> It is the aspect of individual superiority in determination, persistence, endurance, courage; that which determines the quality of action. . . . It is the aspect of leadership we commonly imply in the word "responsibility," the quality which gives dependability and determination to human conducts, and foresight and ideality to purpose.[14]

The Moral Aspect of Leadership

Underlying the survival of formal organization is a complex morality. As pointed out in the preceding chapter, Barnard sees organizations as autonomous ethical systems encompassing contradictory and conflicting moralities.[15]

> Morals are defined as personal forces or propensities of a general and stable character in individuals which tend to inhibit, control, or modify inconsistent immediate specific desires, impulses, or interests, and to intensify those which are consistent with such propensities. This tendency is a matter of sentiment, feeling, emotion, internal compulsion, rather than one of rational processes or deliberation. . . . When the tendency is strong and stable there exists a condition of responsibility.[16]

Morals are private codes of conduct which guide the individual in his

---

[13]*Ibid.*
[14]*Ibid.*, p. 260.
[15]See pp. 106–107.
[16]*The Functions*, p. 261.

behavior and tend to be learned or absorbed from the individual's environment. Generally an individual has learned different codes for different social settings. For example, a man's code of conduct or right behavior as a father and head of a family may be different from his code on the job as an executive or at a party at the country club or as a soldier called up in the army reserves. Since codes of conduct or right behavior involve feelings and emotions and generally exist at a subconscious level they are perceived from the individual's actions rather than his words.

Moral Status Compared with Responsibility

An individual's moral codes are propensities to behave in a certain manner under a specified set of circumstances. These represent the moral status of the individual. They are to be differentiated from responsibility. Responsibility is the measure of the degree to which an individual holds to his code. For example, under adverse circumstances one individual may abandon his private code while another may hold to it. Where the individual holds to his moral code he is acting responsibly. " . . . responsibility is the property of an individual by which whatever morality exists in him becomes effective in conduct."[17]

Since individuals have a number of private codes they may be responsible regarding some and irresponsible with others. It appears, however, that responsibility tends to be a general characteristic, that is, men who are responsible in one respect tend to be responsible in others.

Conflict of Moral Codes

Because an individual usually has several private codes of conduct he is likely to experience conflicts as to what is "right behavior" in a given situation. For example, loyalty to friends may be an important value in one code; yet, an individual holding this belief may at the same time see that his friend is interfering with the good of the organization. In such a setting an individual must resolve the conflict between his obligations for the good of the organization and his duty to personal friends within the organization.

Barnard draws attention to the fact that such conflicts between moral codes is inherent among contributors to an organization. He also notes that the higher one is in the executive hierarchy the more complex and difficult the conflicts will be because a person's codes are a function of the number of organizations to which he is attached and as the number of such attachments increase arithmetically the conflicts tend to increase geometrically. In the executive's case this is illustrated by the constant difficulty he

---

[17]*Ibid.*, p. 267. Emphasis in original.

117

faces in allocating time. Just maintaining the daily schedule of appointments for a high-ranking executive involves conflict of obligations and responsibilities and the problem increases in difficulty as the executive's job is expanded.

Unless properly dealt with conflicts of morals have a debilitating effect on individuals and on formal organization. The problems of numerous unresolved conflicts result in personal frustration, indecisiveness, a decreased sense of general responsibility, and general moral deterioration.

Dealing with Conflicting Moral Codes

How do executives resolve their conflicts with respect to moral and responsible behavior? It should be pointed out that "most frequently the conflict is between organization codes and not between organization and personal codes. . . . "[18] The consequence of failure to deal constructively with such conflict is either the diminution of the sense of responsibility or the destruction of the codes themselves.

It appears that the complexity of the moral situation results in many failures among executives. Most often these arise because of promotion beyond capacity. Men are promoted beyond their ability to find honest solutions and the result is a deterioration of responsibility and morality, especially when appointments are made on the basis of loyalty rather than ability.

It is the importance of the moral issues in Barnard's thinking that led this author to interview him at length to seek more tangible or concrete expression of how he, as a practicing executive, had dealt with conflict of moral codes.

When asked how an executive resolves the conflicts among his multiple codes Barnard answered,

BARNARD: Well, the first thing to say about it is he doesn't know; and if he undertakes to know in the specific instance he will fail. There are an enormous number of things that people have to do on this earth that have to operate just as the physiological system operates, without conscious control. The minute you get conscious about it you lose the control.

WOLF: But still, take your own experience, didn't you ever have to let out a man whom you were personally friendly with, to demote him or retire him or make some decision that put you in a state of conflict between personal loyalty to an individual and loyalty toward the organization? And when you made such a decision did you really just decide on a subconscious basis?

---

[18]*Ibid.*, p. 278.

BARNARD: I would say that that was generally true, yes.

WOLF: Weren't you torn by any feeling of guilt for violating one code of ethics?

BARNARD: I suppose you would be but still you're not conscious of it as being a conflict in a code of ethics. For example, you have a subordinate who's worked nights and Sundays and what not at a scheme that he thinks will be advantageous. He comes to the boss to sell it to him and the reasons supporting his proposals are 1, 2, 3, 4, 5. There's nothing more disconcerting (so disconcerting that I think you can't directly use it too often) than to say to the man "Now Bill, all right, but what's the real reason?" It isn't that he's trying to put something over or that he's really insincere; he never thought of it in those terms. He didn't realize how his personal interest and personal bias were affecting his interest in this particular proposal. Instead he gave all the other rational reasons.

When people are asked to explain their decisions what they give is rationalization. They can't tell the truth because they don't know it, they just don't know how they did operate. They are aware of some things. It's like our awareness of, or failure to be aware of, background, either optical background or auditory background. Ordinarily we have the capacity for shutting that completely out, as you see in its most developed form in textile mills or other places where it is very noisy but where the operators can talk to each other with perfect ease. And yet, let some abnormal condition develop and everybody's alert to it even though they were not listening to it. So much of this question of decisions as to what to do is affected by considerations of that kind. Shall I agree to follow this program or not? Well, my decision may very well depend in the last analysis on the fact that the only person I think could properly operate the program is Bill X, and I can't afford to take Bill X off the job he's doing (which may not be more important than what we are talking about getting him to do but is nevertheless an indispensable function, and I have no one to take his place). You see, the chain spins out and there are a lot of subtle and very complicated things. Now, you ask a man to explain that and he's stuck.[19]

In probing for further specifics on Barnard's ideas for dealing with conflict, this writer asked him about his thinking on the conflict between line and staff units within formal organization. Barnard's response indicated that in most instances the line organization should be supported.

BARNARD: Well, all effective staff work, or most of it at least, is the moral aspect of it. It's persuasive fundamentally. Now it's persuasive

---

[19]*Conversations*, p. 23–24.

partly because whoever is talking is expert in a particular segment, but that is not sufficient. Experts are very frequently quite ineffective because they are unacceptable to line organizations due to overbearing manners, looking down their noses, or what have you. And the top of the organization has to make it work, insofar as they can, by insisting that subordinated line officials take into account what the experts say and advise. In any specific instance the line will always be supported in any good organization. But if in general you find a man in the line organization who doesn't listen to anybody except himself or his boss and who doesn't take into account all the factors and complexes that are involved in practical words, why, you just have to get rid of him. He can't work in the organization, and he's just as bad as the staff man who is really expert in some particular thing but thinks that's the only thing in the world and [that] he has to have his own way about it. No. You get almost an infinite variety of methods by which staff work and line work are conducted. There's no clear-cut division on that subject, and in my opinion there never will be. It depends considerably on personalities.[20]

Another example of Barnard's treatment of conflicting codes is seen in his work with the USO. On one side he was dealing with five religious organizations and the Travelers Aid Society which carried on much of the work. On the other side, he was in constant difficulty with the military authorities who really controlled. Barnard recalled,

> If we sent people out of the country, as we did in the USO camp shows — we gave camp shows all over the world — they had to be cleared by the military. Every individual had to be cleared by the military. Usually that involved another clearance by naval intelligence, and it usually involved clearance by the state department. It got to be a damned complicated business, but I still had to carry on. In the second place there was a lot of information that we needed to manage the thing that we couldn't get, due to the secrecy requirements.[21]

Barnard described how he dealt with the situation:

> The only thing you could do if you had a difficulty was to persuade the military authority that this was something that should be done from the standpoint of military efficiency. You didn't get very far with most military officers in talking about community aspects. The top eschelons would be aware of that, but in a most general way, and wouldn't really know how to apply it. The military authorities are really dependent on the civilians for doing this kind of a job, but they never appreciate it. They did give a good deal of recognition to it, but after it had struggled

---

[20]*Ibid.*, p. 36.
[21]*Ibid.*, pp. 36–37.

through. Initially, when I first went into it, they were just about as cold and frigid as could be — they thought it was just another damnfool organization of do-gooders. You had to fight that kind of thing.[22]

The above are quoted because they illustrate three approaches for dealing with the moral conflict within organizations: by subconsciously acting in terms of a system of priorities so as to not see a conflict and not be caught on the horns of a dilemma; by developing a priority among codes, for example, the line organization ultimately gets the job done so in a crisis over conflicting codes the line organization is usually supported; and by analyzing the situation and restating propositions in order to avoid the conflict.

A final aspect of dealing with conflicting codes is for the executive to be morally creative. The executive needs to inspire morale. "This is a process of inculcating points of view, fundamental attitudes, loyalties to the organization or cooperative system, and to the system of objective authority, that will result in subordinating individual interest and the minor dictates of personal codes to the good of the cooperative whole."[23] Thus the executive influences the moral codes of participants in organizations. He does so by precept, example, teaching, persuasion, appointments, and sanctions. Another way in which the executive deals with moral conflicts is by "inventing a moral basis for the solution of moral conflicts."[24] He either substitutes a new action which avoids the conflict or provides a moral justification for the exception.

Responsibility

If the executive needs to be morally creative, he also needs to maintain executive responsibility. " . . . where creative morality is concerned, the sense of personal responsibility — of sincerity and honesty, in other words — is actually emphasized."[25] Such personal responsibility arises from a deep-seated personal conviction that actions are for the good of the organization. The executive needs to believe in what he does rather than to perform out of fear, obligation, or sanctions. Without conviction executive responsibility diminishes and the participants in the organization also decrease their responsible behavior so as to undermine the cooperative system.

---

[22]*Ibid.,* p. 37.
[23]*The Functions,* p. 279.
[24]*Ibid.,* p. 279.
[25]*Ibid.,* p. 281.

The Sanction of Moral Codes Compared with Responsibility

Since there are a number of moral codes operating in society and since the private codes of individuals may conform with or vary from publicly proclaimed codes, there is a serious problem in determining when a person is behaving responsibly. For example, an observer may judge a man irresponsible for not adhering to a publicly accepted code; whereas for the individual being observed the publicly proclaimed code may not be part of his private code and, therefore, he may in actuality be responsible relative to his own codes. Despite this, responsibility is an important individual quality for it is the characteristic by which private codes of morals become effective in conduct.

It is important to differentiate between sanctions and responsibility. Sanctions may cause people to behave responsibly when in fact they are irresponsible. Moreover, some codes have no specific sanctions associated with them and their observance is a matter of the individual's responsibility. Other codes, usually those associated with behavior in formal organization, involve sanctions. The fear of penalties guides certain aspects of organizational behavior, making such behavior a function more of negative inducements than of moral factors. One needs to make this differentiation because only deeply held convictions give high responsibility, an essential fact for the effective and efficient organization. Without the moral factor organizations lack vitality and tend to disintegrate.

Organization Personality

"Strictly speaking, an organization purpose has directly no meaning for the individual. What has meaning for him is the organization's relation to him — what burdens it imposes, what benefits it confers."[26] In this setting the individual may be thought of as having a dual personality, an individual personality and an organizational one. These may be distinct and different so that while dominated by the organization personality the individual behaves in a way contradictory to his personal motivation (that is, private conduct may be inconsistent with official conduct).[27] The individual's organization personality derives from attachment to formal organization. Adherence to organization morals is a function of the individual's capacity for responsible behavior and the place of organizational codes in the spectrum of personal codes. Where the sense of responsibility is weak it is necessary to rely on sanctions. Where responsibility is great, specific sanctions or incentives will be less important.

---

[26]Ibid., p. 88.
[27]Compare p. 27.

Barnard's Concept of Responsibility Related to the Elements of Organization

For Barnard morals and responsibilities are intimately related to incentives, authority, decisions, and so forth. Essentially he sees the organization as inculcating moral forces into the participants by education, training, selection (associational specialization), informal organization, precepts, examples, and so forth. These are codes of conduct relative to maintaining the zone of indifference respecting objective authority, supporting superiors, attaining organization purposes, being loyal to the organization, accepting policies as guides to decisions, and so forth. Thus, an essence of the functioning organization is its morality as reflected in the moralities of its participants and their sense of responsibility. A critical aspect of executive leadership is dissemination and inculcation of moral codes and development of a sense of responsibility.[28]

In summary the essence of leadership is the creation of moral codes for others. For this to be carried out the executive needs to be sincere. He also needs a sense of conviction, "identification of personal codes and organization codes in the view of the leader,"[29] that is sensed by the informal organization. In other words, where creative morality is involved the executive must believe that what he does is correct. Insincerity is easily recognized by subordinates and leads to demoralization.

A second point is that the endurance of organizations depends upon the quality of leadership and this is intimately related to the question of morality and moral creativeness. The successful executive must lead in the sense of creating an organizational morality that overcomes individual interests, giving meaning to common purpose, creating the incentive that makes other incentives effective, infusing the subjective aspects of decisions with consistence, and inspiring the personal convictions that produce the cohesiveness without which cooperation is impossible.

Underlying all enduring cooperation is a multidimensional and complex morality. While this poses problems of conflict and threatens the survival of organization, the chief factor in mitigating or solving the problem lies in the quality of leadership which is a matter of responsibility, capability, and morality. From the discussion above it should be evident that . . . "among those who cooperate the things that are seen are moved by the

---

[28]In this discussion meanings of responsibility should be carefully differentiated. In the context above responsibility refers to adherence to moral codes. In contrast, responsibility as used in the discussion of delegation of responsibility connotes "acceptance of accountability for a specific or general task."

[29]*The Functions,* p. 281.

things unseen. Out of the void comes the spirit that shapes the ends of men."[30]

Before we leave Barnard's concepts of organization and management, it might be helpful to consider their implications. Just where does Barnard's conceptualization lead? What, if any, beliefs or faith does it support? Barnard answered these questions on the last page of *The Functions of the Executive*:

> This study, without the intent of the writer or perhaps the expectation of the reader, had at its heart this deep paradox and conflict of feelings in the lives of men. Free and unfree, controlling and controlled, choosing and being chosen, inducing and unable to resist inducement, the source of authority and unable to deny it, independent and dependent, nourishing their personalities, and yet depersonalized; forming purposes and being forced to change them, searching for limitations in order to make decisions, seeking the particular but concerned with the whole, finding leaders and denying their leadership, hoping to dominate the earth and being dominated by the unseen — this is the story of man in society told in these pages.
>
> Such a story calls finally for a declaration of faith. I believe in the power of the cooperation of men of free will to make men free to cooperate; that only as they choose to work together can they achieve the fullness of personal development; that only as each accepts a responsibility for choice can they enter into the communion of men from which arise the higher purposes of individual and of cooperative behavior alike. I believe that the expansion of cooperation and the development of the individual are mutually dependent realities, and that a due proportion or balance between them is a necessary condition of human welfare. Beause it is subjective with respect both to a society as a whole and to the individual, what this proportion is I believe science cannot say. It is a question for philosophy and religion.[31]

---

[30]*Ibid.*, p. 284.
[31]*Ibid.*, p. 296.

Appendix 1

Chronological Listing of Articles, Lectures and Manuscripts of Chester I. Barnard*

* This compilation is based upon Barnard's papers and a library search. It was assembled by Professor Haruki Iino of Kansai University, Kyoto, Japan, October 20, 1971 and is printed here with his permission. Great difficulty was encountered in attempting to locate precise reference data on some of Barnard's works. On some all that could be found were his typewritten manuscripts. Hence, the incompleteness of some of the references. Barnard's manuscripts and copies of most of the items shown here are to be found in the Barnard Collection, Baker Library, Harvard University.

1. "An Analysis of a Speech of the Hon. D. J. Lewis Comparing Governmental and Private Telegraph and Telephone Utilities." *Commercial Bulletin* (American Telephone and Telegraph Company, Commercial Engineers' Office) 7 (March 2, 1914): 1–2.

2. "Business Principles in Organization Practice." *Bell Telephone Quarterly* 1 (July 1922): 44–48.

3. "The Development of Executive Ability." Manuscript. Address delivered to (Dean Sackett's) Industrial Conference, Pennsylvania State College, 1925.

4. Untitled talk before Bond Club of New Jersey, October 21, 1927.

5. "Some Problems in the Future Development of New Jersey." Address delivered to Past Presidents of the Camden Chamber of Commerce, Camden, N. J., November 22, 1928.

6. "Significant Telephone Experience in Metropolitan Planning." Address delivered to the Chambers of Commerce of Oranges and Maplewood, N. J., February 27, 1929.

7. "The Basic Work Week." Manuscript. November 1, 1929.

8. "The Interest of Business in Social Progress." Address delivered to the Manufacturers' Association of New Jersey, May 3, 1930.

9. "University Education for Business." A personal letter to Dean Amory R. Johnson, Wharton School of Finance, University of Pennsylvania, September 9, 1930.

10. "Business Integration Essential to Stabilized Progress: An Interview with Chester I. Barnard." *Journal of Industry and Finance*, November 17, 1930, pp. 1–16.

11. "Underlying Factors of Prosperity: An Interview with Chester I. Barnard." *Newark Sunday Call*, January 4, 1931.

12. Address by Chester I. Barnard. February 28, 1931.

13. *Excerpts from Addresses by President Barnard* [from 5, 6, and 12 above]. Newark: New Jersey Bell Telephone Co., 1931.

14. "Why Make Cake Unless We Eat It?" Address delivered to the Newark Business and Professional Women's Club. March 14, 1931. Newark: privately printed, 1931.

15. Untitled Address on Presentation of a Medallion in Recognition of Distinguished Service to the City of Newark during 1931–1932, June 14, 1932.

16. "Men for Affairs." Address delivered to the Faculty and Students of the Wharton School of Finance, University of Pennsylvania, May 14, 1934.

17. "Address before Telephone Organization of Monmouth County, N. J." June 8, 1934. Reprinted in *The New Jersey Bell* 7, Nos. 8 and 9 (1934).

18. *Collectivism and Individualism in Industrial Management.* Address delivered to the Fourth Annual Economic Conference for Engineers, Stevens Institute of Technology Engineering Camp, August 11, 1934. Published from stenographic notes in *The New Jersey Bell* 7 (1934). Reprinted as a pamphlet including numbers 16 and 17 above. Newark: printed privately, 1934.

19. "Some Dangers and Difficulties in the Attainment of Social Security." Address delivered to Monmouth County Organization for Social Service, Brookdale, Red Bank, N. J., September 13, 1934.

20. *Education and Social Welfare.* Address delivered to the Eightieth Annual Convention of the New Jersey State Teachers' Association. November 10, 1934. Newark: printed privately, 1934.

21. "Economic Dependence of Industry upon Education." Address delivered at the National Conference of the Department of Superintendence of the National Education Association, February 26, 1935.

22. "The Purpose of our Learning." Commencement address at State Teachers College, Montclair, N. J., June 15, 1935.

23. "The Cost of Insuring Unemployment Relief." International Claim Association Convention White Sulphur Springs, W. Va., September 9, 1935.

24. "Some Principles and Basic Considerations in Personnel Relations." Address delivered to Fifth Summer Conference Course in Industrial Relations, Graduate College, Princeton University. September 20, 1935. Reprinted in *Organization and Management* [see number 88, below], pp. 3–23.

25. "Public Relief." Address delivered to Convention of New Jersey State League of Municipalities, Asbury Park, N. J., November 14, 1935.

26. *Mind in Everyday Affair: An Examination into Logical and Non-Logical Thought Processes.* Cyrus Fogg Brackett Lecture before the Engineering Faculty

APPENDIX 1

and Students of Princeton University. March 10, 1936. Princeton, N. J.: Princeton University Press, 1936. Reprinted in *The Functions* [see number 45, below], pp. 301–322.

27. "Persistent Dilemmas of Social Progress." Commencement address delivered to the Newark College of Engineering, June 12, 1936.

28. "What Other Purpose?" Commencement address delivered to the Polytechnic Institute of Brooklyn, June 17, 1936.

29. "Twenty-Five Years." The Presidential Address at the Dinner Meeting of the Fifteenth Annual Assembly of the Telephone Pioneers of America, October 23, 1936.

30. Untitled address before the Accountants' Theories and Talk Club of the American Telephone and Telegraph Company, October 28, 1936.

31. "Methods and Limitations of Foresight in Modern Affairs." Address delivered to the Thirtieth Annual Convention of the Association of Life Insurance Presidents, New York, New York, December 4, 1936.

32. "The Employer and Vocational Guidance." Address delivered to the Conference on Vocation Guidance jointly sponsored by the University of Newark and the Jewish Child Guidance Bureau, December 17, 1936.

33. "Some Obscure Aspects of Human Relations." Address delivered before New Jersey State Chamber of Commerce, January 7, 1937.

34. "Some Obscure Aspects of Human Relations." Address delivered before Men's Club of the Munn Avenue Presbyterian Church, January 13, 1937.

35. Untitled address before Newark Young Men's Christian Association Anniversary Luncheon, February 17, 1937.

36. "Notes on Some Obscure Aspects of Human Relations." Manuscript of remarks to Professor Philip Cabot's Business Executive Group at the Harvard Graduate School of Business Administration, March 6, 1937. Includes numbers 33 and 34 above.

37. "Concerning the Theory of Abilities." Manuscript. Appendix to number 36, above.

38. "What Would You Say to the Seniors?" Address delivered to the Twelfth Annual Industrial Conference at Rutgers University, September 9, 1937.

39. "The Functions of the Executive." Manuscript of eight lectures delivered at the Lowell Institute, November 1937.

40. "The Dependence of New Jersey Industry on New Jersey Government." Address delivered to Bamberger Institute, L. Bamberger and Company, Newark, N. J., February 12, 1938.

41. "The Meaning of Loyalty," Address delivered to New Jersey Society of the Sons of the American Revolution, February 22, 1938.

42. "Riot of the Unemployed at Trenton, N. J. 1935. A Case in Concrete Sociol-

127

ogy." Lecture given several times between May 6, 1938, and November 21, 1941, in the course "Sociology 23" under Professor L. J. Henderson at Harvard University. Reprinted with an introduction in *Organization and Management,* pp. 51–79.

43. "Notes Concerning Macaulay's Introduction to his "The Movement of Interest Rates, Bond Yields and Stock Prices in the United States since 1856." Manuscript dated August 1938.

44. "Concerning the Non-Rational in Economic Behavior." Address delivered to the Graduate Economics Club of Columbia University, Men's Faculty Club, Columbia University, November 1, 1938.

45. *The Functions of the Executive.* Cambridge: Harvard University Press, 1938.

46. "Minority Report, the First Fortune Round Table on the Effects of Government Spending upon Private Enterprise." *Fortune,* March 1939. Reprinted as a brochure by *Fortune.*

47. "Non-Rational Economic Action." Address delivered to the Political Economy Club, January 16, 1939.

48. "Dilemmas of Leadership in the Democratic Process." Stafford Little Lecture at Princeton University, March 29, 1939. Reprinted in *Organization and Management,* pp. 24–50.

49. "Rough Notes on the Principles of the Unemployment Problems and its Alleviations." Manuscript dated June 26, 1939. Prepared in connection with correspondence with M. L. Wilson, undersecretary of Agriculture.

50. "Responsibility of the Top Executive for Industrial Relations." Address delivered at Massachusetts Institute of Technology, November 2, 1939.

51. "Observations and Reflections on a Brief Call at Leningrad and Moscow." South Orange, N. J.: printed privately, 1939.

52. "The Relationship of Customers to Business Organizations and Approaches to the Understanding of the Behavior of Executives: Comments on the Job of the Executive." *Harvard Business Review* 18, no. 3 (Spring, 1940): 295–308. Reprinted as "Concepts of Organization" in *Organization and Management,* pp. 111–133.

53. "Collective Cooperation." Address delivered to the Society of Friends, Philadelphia, January 17, 1940.

54. "Nature of Leadership." Address delivered to the Chemical Reserve Officers of the Second Corps Area, January 24, 1940.

55. "Nature of Leadership." Address delivered to Professor Philip Cabot's Week-end Conference of Business Executives, Harvard Graduate School of Business Administration, March 9, 1940.

56. "The Nature of Leadership." In *Organization and Management,* pp. 80–110. Based on numbers 54 and 55, above.

APPENDIX 1

57. "The Significance of Decisive Behavior in Social Action." Manuscript dated April 25, 1940.

58. "Requirements of Leadership in a Democratic Society." Address delivered to Conference of Cooperative Study of Teacher Education, Mt. Summit, Pa., October 24, 1940.

59. *Concerning the Theory of Modern Price Systems and Related Matters.* South Orange, N. J.: privately printed, 1944.

60. "On the Social Significance of Losses." Address delivered to Convention of the New Jersey Bankers Association at Atlantic City, May 23, 1941. Reprinted as "About the Social Significance of Losses." *United States Invester,* May 31, 1941.

61. "Internal Relationships in Industrial Relations Administration." Address delivered to the Industrial Relations Graduate College, Princeton University, September 17, 1941.

62. "Internal Relationships in Industrial Relations Administration." Number 61 was repeated for Northern New Jersey Alumni Association of Massachusetts Institute of Technology, Newark, N. J., April 16, 1942.

63. *How USO Operations are Conducted and Financed: A Report of the President of USO to the Board of Directors.* New York: USO, 1942.

64. *What It Takes to do a Good USO Job: Addressed to Certain Regional Officials of USO.* New York: USO, 1942.

65. "The Deeper Significance of the USO." Address delivered before the National Council, Young Men's Christian Association of the United States, Cleveland, Ohio, October 31, 1942.

66. On Ingenuity and Inventiveness. Comments before the 1942 Annual Meeting of The American Society of Mechanical Engineers.

67. "On Planning for World Government." Address prepared for Conference on Science, Philosophy and Religion, September 1943. Reprinted as "Approaches to World Peace," in *Organization and Management,* pp. 133–175.

68. "Book Review of *The Elements of Administration* by Urwick." *Personnel* 21, no. 4 (January, 1945): 257–258.

69. "Broadcast Over Station WATT, Newark." Manuscript of address delivered for New Jersey State Committee for American Cancer Society, May 17, 1945.

70. "Liberal Education and American Industry." Address delivered to the Conference on The Returning Servicemen and Liberal Education, Princeton University, May 23, 1945.

71. "Functions and Pathology of Status Systems in Formal Organizations." Address delivered to the University of Chicago Human Relations in Industry Seminar, August 15, 1945. Reprinted in *Industry and Society.* William Foote Whyte, ed. New York: McGraw Hill, 1946. Also reprinted in *Organization and Management,* pp. 207–244.

72. "Education for Executives." Remarks at an informal meeting of faculty members of the School of Business and of the Division of Social Sciences of the University of Chicago, August 16, 1945. Reprinted in *Journal of Business of the University of Chicago*, no. 4 (October 1945). Also reprinted in *Organization and Management*, pp. 194–206.

73. "Ethics and Modern Organization." Address delivered before the Bloomfield College and Seminary Convocation Dinner, November 8, 1945.

74. "Book Review of *The Executive in Action* by Marshall E. Dimock." *Political Science Quarterly* 61, no. 1 (March, 1946).

75. "Book Review of *Freedom under Planning* by Barbara Wootton." *The Southern Economic Journal* 21, no. 3 (January, 1964). Reprinted in *Organization and Management*, pp. 176–193.

76. *A Report on the International Control of Atomic Energy*. Washington, D.C.: GPO, 1946. With J. R. Oppenheimer, C. A. Thomas, H. A. Winne, and D. E. Lilienthal.

77. "Atomic Energy Case." Address before Human Relations course under Professor Wallace Donham at Harvard University, April 16, 1946.

78. "Grand Jury Case." Address before Human Relations course under Professor Wallace Donham at Harvard University, April 18, 1946.

79. "International Control of Disarmament." Address before the New York Chamber of Commerce, June 1946.

80. "Memorandum on Modern Problems of Morals and Ethics." Manuscript dated June 1946.

81. "International Control of Atomic Energy." Address before Controllers Institute of America, September 16, 1946. (Reprinted January 1947 for Great Island Conference, N. Y.)

82. "Foreword." In H. A. Simon. *Administrative Behavior: A Study of Decision-Making Processes in Administrative Behavior*. New York: Macmillan, 1958.

83. "Some Aspects of Organization Relevant to Industrial Research." Address before the Twenty-fifth Anniversary of the Industrial Research Department, Wharton School of Finance and Commerce, University of Pennsylvania, January 10, 1947. Reprinted in *The Conditions of Industrial Progress*, pp. 62–72. Philadelphia: Wharton School of Finance and Commerce, University of Pennsylvania, 1947.

84. "Steps to Ease Peril of Extinction Called Unfeasible in U. S." *The Washington Post*, August 3, 1947.

85. "The History and Economics of the Dial Program of the New Jersey Bell Telephone Company." Memorandum for the Supervisory Organization of the Company, September 2, 1947. Reprinted as a brochure with the same title. Newark: New Jersey Bell, 1947.

86. "Atomic Energy Control." Address delivered to the Great Issues Course,

APPENDIX 1

Dartmouth College, December 8, 1947. Reprinted in *Dartmouth Alumni Magazine*, February 1948.

87. "Social Factors in the Medical Career." Address delivered to the Graduate Classes of Medical Divisions, University of Pennsylvania, March 15, 1947. Reprinted in *The General Magazine and Historical Chronicle* [University of Pennsylvania, The General Alumni Society] 50, no. 2 (Winter 1948): 114–120.

88. *Organization and Management.* Cambridge: Harvard University Press, 1948.

89. "Medical Education and Medical Care." Address delivered at the New England Center Hospital, May 26, 1949.

90. "Arms Race v. Control." *Scientific American* 181, no. 5 (November 1949): 11–13.

91. "The President's Review for 1948." In *Annual Report for 1948*. New York: Rockefeller Foundation, 1949.

92. "Skill, Knowledge and Judgment." Commencement address, Massachusetts Institute of Technology, June 9, 1950.

93. "Introductory Lectures in Concrete Sociology, edited with an Introduction." Manuscript dated September, 1950.

94. "Book Review of *Bureaucracy in a Democracy* by Charles S. Hyneman." *American Political Science Review* 44, no. 4 (December 1950): 990–1004.

95. "The President's Review for 1949." In *Annual Report for 1949*. New York: Rockefeller Foundation, 1950.

96. "Basic Elements of a Free, Dynamic Society: A Round-Table Discussion." *Harvard Business Review* 29, no. 6 (November 1951) and 30, no. 1 (January-February 1952).

97. "Science and Organization." In the *Proceedings of the Annual Philosophical Society*, Philadelphia, Pa., November 8–9, 1951.

98. "Foreword." In *Annual Report for 1950*. New York: Rockefeller Foundation, 1951.

99. "Leadership and the Law." In "Symposium: The Relation Between General Education and Law-School Training in the Preparation of a Lawyer." *New York University Law Review* 27, no. 1 (January 1952): 112–116.

100. "Report by the President to the Trustees of The Rockefeller Foundation." Manuscript dated April 2, 1952.

101. "Social Science: Illusion and Reality." *The American Scholar* 21, no. 3 (Summer 1952).

102. "The President's Review for 1950 and 1951." In *Annual Report for 1951*. New York: Rockefeller Foundation, 1952.

103. "Introduction." In *Directory of Fellowship Awards, 1922–1950*. New York: General Education Board, 1951.

104. "Warren Weaver, AAAS President-Elect." *Science* 117, no. 3034 (February 20, 1953): 174–176.

105. "The Elementary Conditions of Formal Organization." Manuscript of informal seminar in operations research, 1953–1954. The Johns Hopkins University, November 3, 1953. Reprinted as seminar paper number 5. Baltimore: Operations Research Office, Johns Hopkins University, 1953.

106. "Elementary Conditions of Business Morals." Barbara Weinstock Lecture on The Morals of Trade at the University of California, Berkley, May 25, 1955. Reprinted in *California Management Review* 1, no. 1 (Fall, 1958): 1–13.

107. "Preface." *The Functions of the Executive.* Japanese ed. 1956.

108. "A National Science Policy." *Scientific American* 197, no. 5 (November, 1957): 45–49.

Appendix 2

Citation to accompany the award of
the Medal for Merit

to

Chester I. Barnard

CHESTER I. BARNARD, for exceptionally meritorious conduct in the performance of outstanding service to the United States as President of the United Service Organizations, Incorporated, from April 29, 1942, to April 13, 1945. In the early days of the USO, when the lack of organization and disunity of the six member agencies were such as to produce a critical situation, Mr. Barnard gave up his duties as President of the New Jersey Bell Telephone Company to assume the presidency of the USO, and for three years devoted himself day and night to its work. Through his executive ability and the force of his personality, the loose federation was given effective organization and operating unity, yet his sense of justice was ever alert to guard the legitimate independence of the agencies from undue encroachment by a unified administration. His sound guidance, his genius for handling complex human relationships, his insistence upon drawing from USO the maximum of service to the men and women of the Armed Forces and to war production workers in the areas of USO responsibility, inspired public approval and an extraordinary degree of public confidence. His awareness of social institutions enabled him both to forestall inappropriate developments and to foresee changing and enlarging aspects of service; and the USO grew under his direction to a well-established and publicly accepted wartime agency, equipped to meet many and varying needs during the greatest period of national emergency. Mr. Barnard's outstanding leadership is in large measure responsible for the success attained by the USO.

(s) Harry S. Truman

Index

Abrams, Frank, 39, 42
Anderson, General Orville, 40
Andrews, Kenneth R., 44
Associational specialization, 74; related to Barnard's friendship with Walter Sherman Gifford, 9
Authority: too much emphasis on, in *The Functions*, 24; related to informal organization, 72; debate between Barnard's view (acceptance theory) and management's right to command, 82; defined, 82–83; of an order, 83–84; pressure to maintain objective, 84; the fiction of superior, 84; precepts regarding, 85–87; responsibility more important than, 85; relationship of, to responsibility, 85–86; limits of the concept that responsibility should be equal to, 86–87; insuring the acceptance of an order, 87–90; related to formal organization, 90, 97

Bach Society of New Jersey, 15
Barnard, Chester I.: summary of contribution to organization and management, 3–4; parents and early life, 5–7; at Harvard, 7–8; as a participant observer, 8; career at American Telephone and Telegraph Co., 8–14; public-spirited activities in New Jersey, 14–15; the writing of *The Functions*, 16–23; impact of publishing *The Functions*, 21–22; writings after publishing *The Functions*, 22–23; experience at the USO, 23–31; Presidential Medal for Merit award, 30, 133; study of older worker in industry, 31; assistant to the Secretary of the Treasury, 31; consultant to U. S. on United Nations Atomic Energy Commission, 33; at the Rockefeller Foundation, 33–34; chairman of the National Science Foundation, 34; service on Hoover Commission, 31; on Committee on Atomic Energy, 31; chairman of Na-

tional Science Board of the National Science Foundation, 34; correspondence with President Dwight Eisenhower, 34–37; improving U. S. relations with the Soviet Union, 38–42; recognition from N. J. Bell Telephone Co., 42–43; death of daughter, Frances, 43; criticism of, at N. J. Bell, 44; humanism, 46–49; general philosophy, 47, 48–49; empiricism, 49–54; books influential on, 49n–50n; letter to John Romanition, 51–52; talk to American Society of Mechanical Engineers, 52; speculative philosophy, 54–55; framework of analysis, 55–59; use of dichotomies in analysis, 55; concept of formal organization, 60–72; goals in writing *The Functions*, 60–61; ideas on the nature of organization, 61–65; the broader environment of organization, 65–71; informal organization, 70–72. Aspects of formal organization: specialization, 73–75; incentives, 76–82; authority, 82–90; decisions, 90–101; status systems, 101–105; organization morals, 106–108. The functions of the executive: providing the organizational communication system, 111–114; formulation of purposes and objectives, 114; executive process, 114–115; executive leadership, 115–121; moral considerations, 116–123; declaration of faith, 124
Barnard, Chester I., writings and speeches: "Business Principles in Organization Practice," summary, 11; "Development of Executive Ability," summary, 11–12; "Education for Executives," 11n; quoted 12, 23n; "Mind in Everyday Affairs," 16, 20, 92; "Methods and Limitations in Foresight in Modern Affairs," 20; "Comments on the Job of the Executive," 22; "Dilemmas of Leadership in the Democratic Process," 22n;

"The Nature of Leadership," 22n; 91n; "Observations and Reflections on a Brief Call at Leningrad and Moscow," 23; "Review of *Freedom Under Planning*," 23n; "International Control of Atomic Energy," 23n; "Atomic Energy Control," 23n; "Functions and Pathology of Status Systems in Formal Organizations," 23n; 101n; "The Elementary Conditions of Business Morals," 23n; 106; 107; "Concerning the Theory of Modern Price Systems and Related Matters," 23n; "Concerning the Modern Price System and Related Matters," 44; "The History and Economics of the Dial Program of the New Jersey Bell Telephone Company," quoted 44; "Some Principles and Basic Considerations in Personnel Relations," 47; "What Other Purpose," 47; unpublished address to Newark Exchange Club, quoted 48–49; "Some Obscure Aspects of Human Relations," 49, 52; "Some Aspects of Organization Relevant to Industrial Research," quoted, 50–51, 64; "Collectivism and Individualism in Industrial Management," 58; "Twenty-five Years," 79; "Review of *The Elements of Administration*," 86–87

Baruch, Bernard, 32, 53

Bentley, Arthur F., *Behavior, Knowledge, Fact*, 49n

Boulding, Kenneth, *The Image*, 1n

Brown, J. F., *Psychology and the Social Order*, 49n

Byrnes, James F., 32–33

Cabot, Philip, 21

Cabrera, Peter J., 45

Causality: in systems of interdependent variables, 50; in society, 53; as a problem in study of organization, 63–64

Choice: as a basis for assuming free will, 69; related to decisions, 90, 91

Clark, John B., 22

Clark, Peter B., and James Q. Wilson,

"Incentive Systems: A Theory of Organization," 76n

Commission on Durable Peace, 37, 38

Committee on Atomic Energy, 32; letter from Secretary of State James F. Byrnes to Barnard regarding report of, 32

Committee on Work in Industry of the National Research Council, *Fatigue of Workers: Its Relation to Industrial Production*, 21n, 89n

Commons, John R., *Institutional Economics*, 49n

Communication: as the principal interlock activity in organization, 64; facilitated by informal organization, 71; to insure acceptance of an order, 87–90; executive organization as a formal system of, 111; need to keep channels as short as possible in, 113. *See also* authority, 82–84; 85–87

Complex causality, 50, 54

Conflict: in complex organizations, 64

Copeland, Melvin, 22

Corporate responsibilities, 107

Dalton, Melville, *Men Who Manage*, 1n, 102n, 112n

Decision: taking risks, 10; Barnard's contribution to, 90; relation of, to other aspects of organization, 90–91; logical and nonlogical thought processes in, 91–96; organizational contrasted with personal, 92, 95; the environment of decision making, 96; the occasion for, 98; evaluation of executive's, 98; opportunistic element in decision making, 99–101; strategic factor in decision making, 100

Determinism, 68–69

Dichotomies used by Barnard in his analysis, 58–59

Dodds, H. W., 18

Donham, W. B., 16

Dulles, John Foster, 37, 38, 49

Economic responsibility, 108

Education for executives. See executive development

Effectiveness: contrasted with efficiency, 69–70

Efficiency: contrasted with effectiveness, 69–70

Ehrlick, Eugene, *The Fundamental Principles of Sociology of Law*, 49n, 83n

Eisenhower, President Dwight, letter to Barnard, 34–35; letter from Barnard, 36; letter to Barnard regarding International Geophysical Year, 36–37

Emerson, Harrington, 3

Empiricism, Chester I. Barnard's, 49–54

Equilibrium, 55

Executive development, 11–12; 50, 94

Executive organization: resulting from necessity for communication, 64; gives wholeness to organization, 64; informal, 112

Executive personnel, 113; qualifications of good executives, 113

Executive process, 114–115

Executive's job: changing the organization, 13; representing the firm; telephone company, 14; related to organization as a whole, 55; limitations from outside, 66; developing, directing, managing, energizing organization, 66, 69; coordination provided by the executive organization, 91; functions of the executive, 111–115; executive process, 114–115; executive leadership, 115–116

Finley, John H., 39

Fisher, R. A., 90n

Ford, Henry, II, 39, 42

Formal organization: defined, 62; composed of activities, 63; as a system, 61–65, 67. Aspects of formal organization: specialization, 73–76; incentives, 76–82; authority, 82–90; decisions, 90–101; status systems, 101–105; organizational morals, 106–107

Formal organization: Barnard's concept of, 58

Forrestal, James, 30

Fosdick, Raymond B., 27; correspond-

ence with John D. Rockefeller, Jr., 28, 33

Free will, 68–69

The Functions of the Executive: translations of, 1, Boulding quote about, 1n. Simon quote about, 1n; writing style in, 2; Barnard's goals in writing, 60–61. Quoted 62, 63; definitions of effectiveness and efficiency in, 70n; quoted on informal organization, 71, 72, 75, 76, 77, 78, 79, 80, 81, 83, 84, 87, 88, 89, 90, 92, 95, 98, 99, 100, 101, 114, 115, 116, 117, 118, 121, 122, 123, 124; unpublished draft of, quoted, 65–66

Gantt, H. L., 3

Gifford, Walter S., 8–9; 33; 42; letter regarding Barnard's portrait, 42–43

Gore, William J., 96n

Henderson, Lawrence J., 1, friendship with Barnard, 16; 18; interest in Vilfredo Pareto, 16, 17–18; invitation to Barnard to give Lowell lectures, 18–20; as chairman of Committee on Work in Industry of the National Research Council, 21; papers edited by Barnard, 23

Hoffman, Paul, 37, 38n

Homans, George C., 1, 21

Homeopathic Hospital, East Orange, New Jersey, 15

Hoover, Herbert, 31

Hoslett, Schuyler D. *Human Factors In Management*, 22–23n

Hospital Council of Essex County, New Jersey, 15

Humanism, Chester I. Barnard's, 46–49

Humphreys, Christmas, *Buddhism*, quoted, 64

Incentives: related to efficiency, 76; complexity of, 76; satisfying existing individual needs (method of incentives), 76, 77–79; changing individual needs (method of persuasion), 76, 77; positive compared to negative, 77; objective, 77; subjective, 77; ineffectiveness of, 77; and specific inducements, 77; general, 77; material, cultivated by society, 77–78; personal, nonmaterial opportunities more important than material, 78; in desirable physical conditions of work, 78; in ideal benefaction, 78; in self-esteem, 78; in developing loyalty, 78–79; limits of method of, 79. Method of persuasion: creation of coercive conditions, 79–80; rationalization of opportunity, 80; inculcator of motives, 80; complexity of incentives, 80–81; dealing with the incentive problem growth, 80; selective recruiting, 80; differentiation a fundamental aspect of incentives, 81–82; personal decision in organization a function of incentives, 97

Individual: distinguish between ability and, 46; respect, 46; Barnard's concept of, 58; as organization participant and as whole person, 67–68; motives, 68; free will and determinism in behavior, 68–69; in relation to informal organization, 71–72

Individualism vs. collectivism, 55–58; 81

Informal organization, 70–71; differentiated from formal, 70; definition of, 70–71; functions performed by informal organization, 71–72; informal executive organization, 112

Intellectual capacity: as part of executive ability, 12, 91

International Geophysical Year, 35, 36

Intuition, 51, 52, 58, 91–96

James, William, 3n

Judgment: in understanding systems of interdependent parts, 50

King, Admiral E. J., 30

Knight, Frank, 90n

Koffka, Kurt, 3; Principles of Gestalt Psychology, 50n

Korzbski, Alfred, Science and Sanity: An introduction to Non-Aristotelian Systems and General Semantics, 49n

Lancaster, Mr. (Quaker leader), 39, 41, 42

Lavine, A. Lincoln, quote of letter on Barnard's contribution to the USO, 31

Leadership: defined, 115–116; moral aspects of, 115–117

Learning: Barnard's, from experience, 49

Legal responsibility, 108

Lewin, Kurt, 90n

Lilienthal Committee. See Committee on Atomic Energy

Lilienthal, David E., 31, 32n

Limitations upon organization from outside, 65–66

Line conflict with staff, 119–120

Linear reasoning, 50

Logical thought processes, 91–96

Lowell, A. Lawrence, 8, 18; letter from Henderson, 19–20; letter to Barnard, 20–21

Lowman, A. A., letter from Barnard, 2n, quoted 6

Loyalty, 78; developing, 79

Malik, J., 38, 39, 40, 41, 42

Malone, Dumas, 19

Management by objectives, 114. See also purpose

Mandeville, Merton J., quoted, 2n

Marshall, General George, 30

Martin, Norman H., "Differential Decisions in the Management of an Industrial Plant," 97n

Mayo, Elton, 21; The Human Problems of Industrial Civilization, 71n

Miller, Spencer, 39–40

Minority groups: integration in the USO, 26

Money: as an incentive, 78; problems of differential income, 78

Mooney, James, 3

Moral basis of organization: illustrated in USO experience, 26; in decision making, 97; seen in an organization as an autonomous moral institution, 106–116; morality defined, 106; varieties in business codes of morality, 106–108; personal compared to representative values, 106–107; moral aspects of leadership, 116–117, 123

Moral codes, 106–107; 116–117; conflict of, 117; dealing with conflicting, 118–121; sanction of, compared with responsibility, 122; complex morality underlying organization, 123; leadership related to morality and moral creativeness, 123

Moral responsibility: based upon assumption of free will, 69

Moral status: compared with responsibility, 117

Motives: needs, 68; complexity of, 68; inferred from what is done, 68

Mount Hermon School, 7

National Science Board, 34, 35, 36

National Science Foundation, 34–37

National War Fund, 26

New Jersey's Emergency Relief: Barnard's role, 14–15

Newark University, 15

Newcomen Society, 16

Nonlogical thought processes, 91–96. *See* intuition

Ogden, C. K., and Richards, I. A., *The Meaning of Meaning*, 49n

Open-system theory, 54, 55

Oppenheimer, Robert, 32

Organization: problem of definition, 21

Organization and Management, 2n, 23n; quoted, 60, 61, 63, 91, 101n, 103, 105, 115

Organization morals. *See* moral basis of organization

Organization structure. *See* specialization; *see also* scheme of organization

Organizational loyalties, 107

Page, Arthur, 19

Pareto, Vilfredo, 3; as a bond of interest between Barnard and Henderson, 16–17; author of *Traité de Sociologie Générale*, 17; Henderson's polemic position on, 23, 49n; and causality in systems of interdependent variables, 50

Pearson, Karl, 90n

Perkins, Frances, 31

Personality: personal compared with organizational, 92; of organization, 122

Personnel loyalties, 107

Personnel relations: development of the individual as of first importance, 47

Pessimism, contrasted with defeatism, 53

Philosophizing, value of, 59

Pickett, Clarence, 38, 39

Pierce, J. R., 45

Purpose: the coordinating and unifying principal of formal organization, 65; unifying element and contrast of general to specialized, 75–76; the executive function of formulating, 114; relationship of, to assignment of responsibility, 114

Reck, Dickson, "The Role of Company Standards in Industrial Administration," 97n

Reeder, William O. *Variations on a Theme by Barnard*, 2n

Responsibility: relationship to authority, 85; need to develop the subject of, 85n; limits of concept that authority should be equal to, 86–87; relationship to morals, 106; personal, compared with representative or official, 106–107; assignment of, the critical aspect of formulation of purpose, 114; compared with moral status, 117; executive, 121; sanction of moral codes compared with, 122; related to moral behavior, 122; related to the elements of organization, 123; contrasted with accountability, 123n

Rockefeller, John D., Jr., 26; letter to Barnard, 27; letter from Raymond B. Fosdick, 28; letter to Raymond B. Fosdick, 28; letter to Barnard, 29; letter to Barnard, 29–30

Roethlisberger, F. J., and Dickson, W. J., *Management and the Worker*, 71n

Romanition, John: letter to, from Barnard, 50–51

Rusk, Dean, 34; 39

Scheme of organization, 112

Securing of essential services as an executive function, 113–114

Selander, Fred S., 96n

Self-esteem in relation to incentives, 78–79

Selznick, Philip, 1n

Simon, Herbert: 1, *Administrative Behavior*, 1n; 90n; on political democracy, 47; letter to, from Barnard quoted, 59; influence of Barnard on, in decision making, 90n; letter from, to William B. Wolf, quoted, 90n, 96, 97n

Soviet Union: Barnard's involvement in improving U. S. relations with, 38–42

Specialization: to determine effectiveness of cooperative systems, 73; primary aspect of, derives from purpose, 73; five lines of, 73; temporal, 73–74, associational, 9; 74; functional, 73; process, 73; autonomous nature of units of, 74–75

Staff: Barnard's experience, 11

Status systems: omission from *The Functions*, 24; general nature of, 101–102; functional status compared with hierarchial status, 102; devices used to establish, 102–103; functions of, 103–104; disruptive tendencies of, 104–105

Steady state, 55. *See* also equilibrium

Steiner, George A., "How to Forecast Defense Expenditures," 97n

Stimson, Henry L., 30

Strategic factor: theory of, 100, 101

System, formal organization as a system, 62–65

Sunny, B. E., 10

Tannenbaum, Robert, "The Management Concept," 1n; "Management Decision Making," 97n

Taussig, Frank W., 8

Taylor, Frederick, W., 3

Technical responsibility, 108

Telephone Pioneers of America, 16

Thomas, A. Charles, 32n

Training, executive. *See* executive development

Thayer, H. B., 10

United Service Organization USO, 23–31

University of Chicago, 16

Urwick, Lyndall, 3; *The Elements of Administration*, 86–87

Watson, T. J., 30

Welsh, Frances Barnard, daughter of Chester I. Barnard, 43, 44

Wheeler, William Morton, 18n

Whitehead, Alfred North, *Process and Reality*, 49n; 50n; 59

Whitehead, T. N., *Leadership in a Free Society*, 71n

Whyte, William F.: *Industry and Society*, 23n; letter to, from Barnard, 53; 101n

Willits, Dr., 38

Wilson, Charles E., 39, 40, 41, 42

Winne, Harry A., 32n

Wolf, William B.: Unpublished Interview with Chester I. Barnard, quoted, 8, 16; "Precepts for Managers," quoted, 79; "Organization Constructs: A Guide to Understanding Organizations," 62n; *Management: Readings Toward a General Theory*, 62n; *Conversations with Chester I. Barnard*, quoted, 5, 6, 7, 8, 9, 10, 13, 14, 16, 18, 22, 23, 24, 25, 26, 34, 85, 86, 93, 94, 96, 115, 119, 120, 121

Wooton, Barbara, 23n

Zone of indifference, 83–84